There are many voices in the BRI world, not all of which are really helpful. Loran has written a very thoughtful, principle-driven book that I believe will add much to this necessary conversation about what a believing investor should know about applying their faith to all investing decisions. I believe this book will be around for many years. I recommend it very highly.

RON BLUE, FOUNDING DIRECTOR OF KINGDOM ADVISORS, AND BEST-SELLING AUTHOR OF EIGHTEEN BOOKS ON FINANCE FROM A BIBLICAL PERSPECTIVE, INCLUDING *MASTER YOUR MONEY*.

I believe in Biblically Responsible Investing (BRI). If my money is really God's money, and if God is good and holy, shouldn't I invest his money in companies that offer a good service or product? Shouldn't I avoid investing in businesses that take advantage of human weaknesses by tempting people to sin, self-destruction, and disintegration of the family? In *Investing with Integrity*, Loran Graham has put together a clear, engaging, and persuasive case for BRI. I encourage you to look at it carefully and to ask God what he wants you to do with the money He has entrusted to your care.

RANDY ALCORN, AUTHOR OF *MONEY, POSSESSIONS & ETERNITY*, *THE TREASURE PRINCIPLE* AND *MANAGING GOD'S MONEY*

Loran Graham has done a superb job in *Investing with Integrity* to help followers of Christ align their investment decisions with the heart of God. How we handle money is so important to the Lord that there are 2,350 verses in the Bible dealing with it. You will be challenged and encouraged as you learn God's way of investing. I heartily recommend this book!

HOWARD DAYTON, FOUNDER OF COMPASS—FINANCES GOD'S WAY™ (WWW.COMPASS1.ORG)

Wise stewardship isn't just about saving, investing, and avoiding debt—it's about doing so in a way that honors the Lord. Loran Graham's book provides readers with a comprehensive strategy for doing just that, through Biblically Responsible Investing.

JIM DALY, PRESIDENT OF FOCUS ON THE FAMILY

One can't take discipleship seriously without understanding stewardship, and investing is an integral element of financial stewardship. *Investing with Integrity* ventures far beyond the topic of investing; it lays out a paradigm for biblical financial stewardship. As Christian investors, we have a fiduciary duty to know how the Owner wants us to invest His money. Loran candidly shares the story of his own growth journey while giving a balanced overview of the different voices on Biblically Responsible Investing. This is a must-read, not only for Christian financial professionals, but for all Christian investors.

CHRIS GOULARD, CFP ®, PASTOR OF STEWARDSHIP FOR SADDLEBACK CHURCH; CHAIRMAN OF CHRISTIAN STEWARDSHIP NETWORK

Investing with Integrity paints a clear, grace-filled picture of how investment decisions fit into the bigger picture of biblical stewardship. Through the lens of his own personal journey, Loran Graham takes a long view of history, from Main Street to Wall Street, in an approachable, story-filled narrative that illustrates the heart story behind Biblically Responsible Investing. Our investments can truly impact the kingdom.

DAVID WILLS, CEO OF THE NATIONAL CHRISTIAN FOUNDATION

This book matters because Loran Graham presents a compelling case for lining up our finances with our Christian convictions. Specifically, he argues for reconciling our investments with our beliefs. He's clear and passionate without being judgmental. He explains how new levels of technical sophistication make screening our investments possible. Without question, Graham offers faithful and shrewd financial advice, but when I let financial investing be a metaphor for my time and work investments, the book becomes flat-out compelling, both a reproach and an inspiration. If you're interested in aligning your portfolio or your life with your beliefs, you need to read this book.

DR. BILL ROBINSON, PRESIDENT EMERITUS OF
WHITWORTH UNIVERSITY; AUTHOR OF *LEADING PEOPLE FROM THE
MIDDLE: THE UNIVERSAL MISSION OF MIND AND
HEART AND INCARNATE LEADERSHIP*

It is rare that someone who is in the day-to-day rigors of their profession can see with vision the big picture of both their clients' wishes and the integration of a Christian worldview. Loran has been able to do this, and with additional insight he brings other resources into this book and gives proper credit to many contributors in the field of Biblically Responsible Investing. Investors will benefit from reading this book, as he has brought a new level of understanding to faith-based investors.

DWIGHT SHORT, AUTHOR OF *KINGDOM GAINS* AND
PROFIT OR PRINCIPLES

My friend Loran Graham wrote from the heart when he wrote *Investing with Integrity*. As one of the emerging statesmen in the Biblically Responsible Investing movement, Loran shares insights and principles about investing in an encouraging yet challenging manner. From my perspective, if God is the Owner of all our money and investments (and He is), shouldn't we invest His money in a way that would please Him as the Owner? If you want to honor God in how you invest your (His) money, read this book. And then…invest with integrity!

JEFF ROGERS, CO-FOUNDER AND CHIEF INSPIRATION OFFICER OF
STEWARDSHIP ASSET MANAGEMENT

This powerful and concise book by Loran Graham will enlighten and challenge Christian believers in this critically important area of life—stewardship. Regardless of where you are in your own investment journey, investing God's resources according to His wishes is not something any of us dare take lightly. When Jesus used the phrase, "Well done, good and faithful slave," He was referring to how these stewards invested what they had been entrusted with. If you want to someday hear, "Well done," you need to read this book and then apply it!

E.G. JAY LINK, PRESIDENT OF STEWARDSHIP MINISTRIES AND KARDIA

Christianity Today once said that I wrote the first book outlining the scriptural basis for an evangelical embrace of responsible investing. Twenty years later, it should say that Loran has written the best book on the subject.

GARY MOORE, AUTHOR OF *FAITHFUL FINANCES 101* AND
*SPIRITUAL INVESTMENTS: WALL STREET WISDOM FROM
THE CAREER OF SIR JOHN TEMPLETON*

LORAN GRAHAM

INVESTING
WITH
integrity

Investing With Integrity
Copyright 2014 © Loran Graham, CPA, CFP®

Published by Deep River Books
Sisters, Oregon
www.deepriverbooks.com

Unless otherwise indicated, all Scripture quotations are taken from the *Holy Bible,* NEW INTERNATIONAL VERSION, copyright © 1973, 1978, 1984 International Bible Society. Used by permission of Zondervan Bible Publishers.

Scripture quotations designated "ESV" are taken from *English Standard Version.* Copyright © July 2001 by Crossway Books/Good News Publishers, Wheaton, IL, tel: 630/682-4300, www.goodnews-crossway.org.

Scripture quotations designated "NASB" are taken from the *New American Standard Bible,* © 1960, 1962, 1963, 1968, 1971, 1972, 1973, 1975, 1977, by the Lockman Foundation, LaHabra California. Used by permission.

Scripture quotations designated "NLT" are taken from the *Holy Bible, New Living Translation,* copyright © 1996. Used by permission of Tyndale House Publishers, Inc., Wheaton, Illinois 60189. All rights reserved.

Scripture quotations designated "NRSV" are taken from the *New Revised Standard Version Bible.* Copyright © 1989, Division of Christian Education of the National Council of the Churches of Christ in the United States of America. Used by permission. All rights reserved.

ISBN – 13: 9781940269139
ISBN – 10: 194026913X

Library of Congress: 2013957335
Printed in the USA
Cover design by David Litwin, Pure Fusion Media

IMPORTANT DISCLOSURES

The opinions voiced in this material are for general information only and are not intended to provide specific advice or recommendations for any individual. To determine which investment(s) may be appropriate for you, consult your financial advisor prior to investing. All performance referenced is historical and is no guarantee of future results. All indexes are unmanaged and may not be invested into directly.

This material and the BRI approach are based on an interpretation of biblical principles. You and others may not agree with all of the interpretations the author presents.

Stock investing involves risk, including loss of principal.

Investing in mutual funds involves risk, including possible loss of principal.

Returns may be lower with Biblically Responsible Investing than if the adviser made decisions based solely on other investment considerations, but they could also be higher.

Investors should consider the investment objectives, risks, charges, and expenses of the investment company carefully before investing. The prospectus and, if available, the summary prospectus contain this and other important information about the investment company. You can obtain a prospectus and summary prospectus from your financial representative. Read carefully before investing.

There is no guarantee that a diversified portfolio will enhance overall returns or outperform a non-diversified portfolio. Diversification does not protect against market risk.

Indexes are unmanaged and cannot be invested into directly. Unmanaged index returns do not reflect fees, expenses, or sales charges. Index performance is not indicative of the performance of any investment. Past performance is no guarantee of future results.

The information that appears in this book is for educational purposes only and does not constitute a solicitation to buy or sell any security. All marks, brands, and names belong to the respective companies and manufacturers and are used solely to identify the companies and products.

Certified Financial Planner Board of Standards Inc. owns the certification marks CFP®, Certified Financial Planner™ and federally registered CFP (with flame design) in the US, which it awards to individuals who successfully complete CFP Board's initial and ongoing certification requirements.

ACKNOWLEDGMENTS

My deepest thanks to…

The Lord, who gave me life and the ability to write. All glory, honor, and praise to Him alone.

My wife, who loves me for who I am. Without her support, none of this would be possible.

My parents, who taught me to value hard work and never to give up on my dreams.

All the clients we serve, for their loyalty, support, and encouragement. Without our clients, none of this would have been possible.

R. Scott Rodin, for his friendship and the countless hours he invested as a mentor and coach throughout the writing process.

Ron Blue, for his inspirational leadership, extraordinary faith, and friendship.

Randy Alcorn, for his friendship, trust, and wise counsel in navigating the publishing process.

Dr. Bill Robinson, for giving me the courage to embark on this project.

Chris Rodgers, CRU City, for providing the tools to help communicate my personal testimony effectively.

Dan Hardt, Robin John, Rusty Leonard, Jay Link, Jeff Rogers, Dwight Short, Tom Strobhar, and Keith Weir, for their wisdom, interviews, and helpful insights.

My close friend David M. Block, who has been an encouragement every step of the way.

Neil Zeigler, for introducing me to Kingdom Advisors and for his friendship along my faith journey.

Jim and Cheryl Strandy, for their support and help brainstorming book titles on the ski lift.

Pastor Jerry Kennedy, for his encouragement and valuable feedback, and for affirming that the theology referenced in this book is sound.

My office assistant, Kristi Tuomala, for providing the organizational support to help make this book possible.

Brian Smith, for his talented editing, coaching, and dedication to help get this book where it needed to be for maximum kingdom impact.

David Mitchell and his team at Interactive Consulting, for their artistic design work and thoughtful approach to the graphic illustrations in the book.

Bill Carmichael, Kit Tosello, and the entire team at Deep River Books for helping to make this book a reality.

CONTENTS

FOREWORD

Imagine you are serving on a jury, listening to the testimony of a key witness. As he tells his story in great detail, you attend carefully to make sure his testimony is consistent. Suddenly, he says something that seems to directly contradict almost everything he has shared to that point. You watch as the prosecuting attorney jumps to his feet and calls the witness on the inconsistency. The witness stammers and stumbles and is not able to explain the incongruity in the story.

What is your reaction? In a court of law, one significant contradiction calls into question the integrity and truth of the entire story. You would ask yourself, "If this part of the testimony doesn't line up with everything else, can we really believe anything he said?"

This is the challenge of the Christian life. When we proclaim that we are followers of Jesus Christ, we commit to a set of values that must be lived out consistently across all areas of life. When we engage in actions, decisions, or attitudes that don't align with those values, we are labeled as hypocrites. Yet as sinners we know how difficult it is to live a life consistently aligned with values of the kingdom of God. Thankfully, God forgives us when we veer from the path. But what about those places that we've never even considered—places that, once examined, prove to contain glaring inconsistencies? Can we become so accepting of the world's values that we make decisions in some areas of life without considering how our faith should guide and shape those decisions?

In this winsome and challenging book, Loran Graham shines a light on just such decisions regarding our choice of investments. Over the last decade we have seen an unprecedented movement toward a better understanding of what it means to be a faithful steward of God's resources, including creation itself. However, in all that progress, there has been precious little said about using our Christian values to guide the ways we *invest* those resources. It is rare indeed that we are challenged to think about the implications of investing in companies whose values are in direct conflict with our own.

That is why I believe this book is such a valuable contribution to the field of stewardship. Loran has combined his deep personal faith with his professional training and expertise in financial management to provide us with a roadmap for a different type of investing journey. He does not demand, judge, or berate; rather, he gently and lovingly invites and challenges us to consider the implications when we claim to follow Jesus while investing His funds in companies whose activities contradict the values of His kingdom.

Much of what you will read here might make you uneasy, and that's the point. We have not been challenged to think through the consistency of our witness as it applies to this area of our lives. So often the way in which we invest our money seems far removed from the "spiritual" part of our lives. Postmodern philosophy tells us that such inconsistency is acceptable and even beneficial. However, we are called to reject the lure of the unexamined life and embrace instead the level of obedience that places every component of life under the light of grace and truth. Loran helps turn that light on, to an area that has remained in the darkness far too long.

The good news is that there exists an excellent alternative to investment-as-usual. Biblically Responsible Investing provides followers of Jesus Christ the opportunity to invest with confidence and joy, knowing that the resources God has entrusted to us are at work in companies whose values reflect our own. Every Jesus follower should consider this opportunity!

I pray that you will read this book with an open mind and heart—open to the Spirit's working in you, open to taking steps that bring greater consistency to your life's witness. The result will be not only your own inner peace, but also the channeling of investment funds into businesses that contribute positively to our society and that further biblical values in their policies, operations, and culture. A double blessing for the kingdom of God.

My thanks to Loran for giving me the opportunity to write this foreword and to work with him on the development of this book. If you follow his lead, I believe you will be richly blessed.

R. SCOTT RODIN , PHD, PRESIDENT OF RODIN CONSULTING INC.
AUTHOR OF *THE STEWARD LEADER*, *THE SOWER*, AND
THE THIRD CONVERSION

INTRODUCTION

> Few things are more infectious than a godly lifestyle.
> The people you rub shoulders with everyday need that
> kind of challenge. Not prudish. Not preachy. Just spot-
> on clean living. Just honest-to-goodness, bone-deep,
> nonhypocritical integrity. Authentic obedience to God.[1]
>
> DR. CHARLES R. SWINDOLL

We all have turning points in our lives—those watershed
moments that significantly change us. In many ways, this book
is about a key turning point in my life and career. Let me say
from the beginning that I am not a pastor nor do I have any formal training in theology. In fact, my professional training is in
finance and investing. This is simply a story about my journey,
and how my story fits into a larger Story. I believe God is up to
something in history.

A BUSINESS PROPOSITION

Suppose you were presented with an offer to purchase a strip
club, which covered for an underground prostitution ring, as a
surefire way to make money. What would you say? A true
Christ-follower would say no in the blink of an eye. This clear
conviction of right and wrong does not flow from legalistic self-
righteousness, but rather from a sense of love and compassion.
We feel compassion for the employees because this enterprise
would be degrading to women, whom God created in His
image to be honored and lifted up. We feel compassion for
those who would patronize the business out of human weakness. Such sex-focused "businesses" fill our hearts with lustful
temptation and demean sexuality to its basest level instead of
preserving it as a sacred gift between husband and wife. We

would say no because, in the end, God gives us His good commandments not to harm us but to protect us, out of His great love and compassion.

Now suppose you could be a 10-percent silent partner in the strip club and never step foot in the place. Would you still say no? Would it make a difference if your ownership were only 1 percent? Chances are, the answer is still no. You see, when we are talking about direct private ownership of a business, these choices are clear for the Christian believer.

But what if we did not know where our investment dollars were going? What if the investment were a mysterious black box that we put money into and profits came out? The moral question gets a bit fuzzy when you don't have enough information to evaluate the morality of the investment. That's how most people feel about certain types of investments—like mutual funds—where the investor may be multiple steps removed from the actual business enterprises to which he or she is contributing money. In cases like this, it helps to break things down to their most basic elements. Simply put, owning a share of stock means that you own a small piece of a company. And owning a share of a mutual fund means you own small pieces of many companies, with a fund manager between you and those companies, making it easier for you to remain ignorant of those companies' activities.

My point is this: ownership carries with it a moral responsibility. Stock or mutual fund ownership is fundamentally no different from any other business or partnership. There are risks associated with stock and mutual fund ownership, just like owning a business, including the loss of your principal. Of course, we could review all the legal and tax implications that make stock ownership different. But this is not an accounting book, so we will not venture into that level of detail. What we're talking about here is the realm of biblically-based morality in business ownership, and in that respect stock or mutual fund ownership carries with it the same responsibility as any other business ownership.

When I made that connection, that's when I really woke up to the importance of this ownership responsibility. This book is written primarily to the faithful steward who has made the decision to follow Jesus Christ, who is seeking to honor the Lord in every area of his or her life, and who has money to invest for the future. If that describes you, then let us explore together what it means to invest with integrity. The word *integrity* actually stems from the Latin word for "integer," meaning whole or complete.[2] In ethical terms, it means a consistency of character and actions. Integrity is about living a life that is wholly in alignment to your values, beliefs, and principles. It's about being all-in.

As Christ followers, we are called to honor God in all that we do. Biblically Responsible Investing (BRI) may be described simply as an opportunity to pursue gains in the stock market without compromising conscience. For the individual investor, BRI represents an opportunity to make sure the ways we invest and save for the future are aligned to our faith and values, as an extension of our ongoing, vital act of daily worship (see Romans 12:1). And on a collective level, imagine if all Christian believers aligned their investments this way. Together, the Christian community has an opportunity to influence corporate behavior and culture as Biblically Responsible Investing reaches a critical mass of participation (which we will discuss later in the book).

Until recently, there was really no way to know what companies or causes we were supporting when it came to investing in the stock market through mutual funds. Now, BRI provides an opportunity to peek inside the black box and make sure the companies we own as investors are in alignment with our Christian values.

> Ethics and spiritual principles should be the basis of everything we do in life. All that we say, all that we think. Every activity should be based on that, including selection of investments.

> SIR JOHN TEMPLETON

Keep in mind that BRI is not a prosperity-gospel magic lamp that will somehow bless all investing activity. If you hear promises to that effect in the investment business, whether faith-based or not, run as fast as you can in the opposite direction! When it comes to investing, there is no silver bullet. There is, however, biblical wisdom in following a principled approach. Proverbs 13:11 says, "Wealth gained hastily will dwindle, but whoever gathers little by little will increase it." All investing involves risk and potential loss of *principal* (money), which is why risk management and diversification are so important. Investing does not, however, require the loss of *principle* (integrity, character).

BRI represents a framework to help investors avoid companies that profit from activities that are not honoring to God. Further, it is entirely possible to adopt the BRI framework within a well-diversified portfolio designed to help you pursue your needs and future goals.* Of course, it is possible that returns may be lower with Biblically Responsible Investing than if the investor made decisions based solely on other investment considerations, but they could also be higher. We will discuss this further in Chapter 5, "Myth Busting." A competent financial advisor who is knowledgeable about BRI—whether or not he or she shares your faith—will be able to help educate and guide you in planning a strategy that is right for you, based on your

---

*There is no guarantee that a diversified portfolio will enhance overall returns or outperform a non-diversified portfolio, and diversification does not protect against market risk.

individual needs and objectives. And if your financial advisor does share your Christian faith, you've found a helper who's even better equipped to align faith and financial strategy by translating Christian values into specific investment goals.

The purpose of this book is not to guilt or shame Christians into thinking in terms of Biblically Responsible Investing. The call to action in this book is simply this: Search the Scriptures in prayer. Talk with your pastor and financial advisor about BRI. And be faithful to what God is teaching you in this area.

This book was born out of a desire to find a resource for my clients that describes Biblically Responsible Investing—the story of its development and what it is all about. After searching extensively, I began to feel a gentle nudge at my heart asking, *Why don't you write a book?* To explore the possibility, in May 2012, I had coffee with my new friend, Dr. Bill Robinson, president emeritus of Whitworth University. I confessed that I felt unworthy to write a book like this. To my surprise and initial dismay, Bill said, "You're right!" Then he reminded me of the story of Jesus calling Simon Peter in Luke 5:8. When Jesus asked Peter to follow him, Peter fell down at Jesus' feet and said, "I'm not worthy, Lord, because of my sin." It was precisely at the point when Peter acknowledged his unworthiness that Jesus replied, "Do not be afraid. From now on, you will be a fisher of men." Bill reminded me that God chooses the weak to demonstrate His power. We are all unworthy, so it's all the more amazing that God uses us to advance His work and His love in the world.

What makes this nation great is freedom—freedom of religion, freedom of speech, and economic freedom in the marketplace. We live in a country that is rich in cultural and religious diversity, because our forefathers envisioned a land where communities would be free to practice what they believed in peace and harmony, and to pursue economic opportunity for a better life. For the Christ follower, BRI presents not a legalistic requirement, but an opportunity to exercise one's religious freedom in the realm of finance, an opportunity for alignment between faith and life practice. BRI is not about guilt or judgment. Rather, it is about obedience and joy in response to God's unconditional love and the gospel of grace.

> For Christ's love compels us, because we are convinced that one died for all, and therefore all died. And he died for all, that those who live should no longer live for themselves but for him who died for them and was raised again.
>
> 2 CORINTHIANS 5:14–15

As we explore the BRI concept together, my hope is that we approach the throne of Truth with humility, love, and grace. With anticipation of joy, not obligatory pressure. BRI is an attempt to demonstrate God's love and compassion in the world by choosing to invest in companies that are honoring to Him, and by avoiding those which do not honor Him or which are harmful to society. Sir John Templeton (1912-2008) is largely credited as being one of the greatest investors of all time, and was perhaps one of the early pioneers in the concept of aligning investment to values. In Gary Moore's book, *Spiritual Investments: Wall Street Wisdom from the Career of Sir John Templeton*,[3] he quotes Templeton:

> Ethics and spiritual principles should be the basis of everything we do in life. All that we say, all that we think. Every activity should be based on that, including selec-

tion of investments. You wouldn't want to be the owner of a company that is producing harm for the public, and therefore, you wouldn't want to be the owner of a share of a company that is producing harm for the public. We should all give great attention to that, and probably it will be profitable to you, because companies that are harmful ordinarily do not prosper for very long. You will be better off with companies that are truly beneficial.

BRI is not about passing judgment on a company or its leaders. After all, I too am part of the fallen crowd. In 1 Corinthians 13:1–2, Paul wrote, "If I speak in the tongues of men and of angels, but have not love, I am only a resounding gong or a clanging cymbal. If I have the gift of prophecy and can fathom all mysteries and all knowledge, and if I have a faith that can move mountains, but have not love, I am nothing." In writing this book, my hope is that I am not a clanging cymbal, as the apostle Paul warned, but rather a helpful marker along the road.

I have come to understand that we are all sojourners in life. Someone once asked Billy Graham what it was like to be one of the great evangelists of our time. Billy Graham responded, "Look, I'm just a beggar, telling other beggars where to find the bread." It's this kind of humility with which I offer this book.

What This Book Seeks to Accomplish

We cannot hold a torch to light another's path without brightening our own.

Ben Sweetland

As we explore BRI together, my hope for the reader is that the exercise will help expand your view of biblical stewardship in a new way, just as my discovery experiences did for me. My hope for this book is to provide a resource, not only for the church and the investing public, but also for other financial advisors to communicate with their clients and firms about the opportunity BRI presents.

The Bible refers to us as stewards or managers of all the resources God has entrusted to us. We and everything in our keeping—our time, our health, our abilities, our opportunities, our wealth and material possessions—belong to Him, and we are accountable to handle them according to His wishes. This book focuses on our stewardship of money—the God-given guidelines for our spending, saving, giving, and lifestyle decisions. One aspect of financial stewardship involves our saving and investment for the future.

With these dynamics in mind, let us imagine financial stewardship as a *Three-Story House*. Proverbs 24 says, "By wisdom a house is built, and through understanding it is established; through knowledge its rooms are filled with rare and beautiful treasures" (verses 3–4).

FAITH IN CHRIST
Called To Be A Steward

FOUNDATION

In building any house, first you must start with a solid foundation. And the *Foundation* of the stewardship House begins with faith in Christ. Other key concepts that make for a firm Foundation include believing that God owns it all, that His perspective is eternal, and that God is our provider and protector. All of these convictions, mixed together, are the concrete used to pour a reliable Foundation on which to build a biblical stewardship model. We will discuss more about the Foundation in Chapter 1, "Laying the Foundation."

1 STEWARDING
Relationships

FIRST STORY

Teacher, which is the greatest commandment in the Law? Jesus replied: "Love the Lord your God with all your heart and with all your soul and with all your mind. This is the first and greatest commandment. And the second is like it: Love your neighbor as yourself. All the Law and the Prophets hang on these two commandments."

MATTHEW 22:36–40

Once we have a solid Foundation in place, we can begin construction on the *First Story*. The First Story relates to how we steward our relationships with God and with others. This dynamic is perhaps most eloquently summarized in Jesus' teaching on the greatest commandments, which I've quoted above. A pastor once told me that only three things in this world are eternal: God, His Word, and His people. If we are to live our lives from an eternal perspective, wouldn't we want to invest our time and other resources in things that last? That's what the First Story is all about.

When we first enter a house, it's typically through the front door. (And for sake of this illustration, let's assume the front door is always located on the First Story.) Jesus says to believers, "Behold, I stand at the door and knock. If anyone hears my voice and opens the door, I will come in to him and eat with him, and he with me" (Revelation 3:20, ESV). Our relationship to the Lord and toward others is the starting point of our faith journey. Perhaps this is why the First Story is in closest proximity to the foundation. If the Second and Third Stories relate to how we manage money, perhaps the First Story is best described as an expression of how we manage our time (although other types of resources certainly come into play in our relationships).

2 STEWARDING
Resources

Avoiding Debt

Giving

Saving

Lifestyle Decisions

Be sure you know the condition of your flocks, give careful attention to your herds; for riches do not endure forever, and a crown is not secure for all generations.

PROVERBS 27:23–24

The *Second Story* relates to how we spend money. I love the wisdom of Proverbs 27 quoted above. In ancient times, society and commerce were centered around agriculture and land ownership. Wealth back then was measured not in shares of stock, but quite literally in the quantity and quality of livestock and fields. The underlying principle is timeless and still applies today. We are called to take careful responsibility for the resources entrusted to us, otherwise there is a real danger those blessings may be squandered.

In the early 1990s, Ron Blue, founding director of Kingdom Advisors, was called to give expert testimony before the United States Senate to share some of his wisdom regarding financial principles. His firm, Ronald Blue and Company, was at the time—and still is—the largest Christian-focused financial planning firm in the nation. Blue, one of three panelists to participate in the discussion, was invited by Senator Coats of Indiana and by Senator Dodd of Connecticut, who moderated as chairman of the committee. When asked what he would tell the typical American family about finances, Blue responded that four key principles have consistently guided his advice:

1. Spend less than you earn.
2. Avoid the use of debt.
3. Maintain liquidity.
4. Think long-term.

After a pause, Senator Dodd replied, "Mr. Blue, it would seem to me that these principles could be applied at any income level."

To which Blue politely added, "Yes, Senator, including the United States government!"

If only our own government had followed these four principles over the past twenty years, perhaps the national debt would not be over 17 trillion dollars today, and counting. Through my Kingdom Advisors membership, I have learned that there are five ways you can spend money. Here they are, listed in order of priority:

- Give it away.
- Pay taxes.
- Make debt payments.
- Save or invest for the future.
- Pay lifestyle expenses.

The order of these categories is important. In contrast, consumer society teaches us always to put *lifestyle* first, and to compound that error by using debt to leverage lifestyle even more through "zero-interest" financing and credit cards. As a result, no money is left over at the end of the month for giving or saving. Under this model, life quickly becomes a struggle just to stay above water as debts begin to mount.

The Second Story of our stewardship house is built from principles that help us properly order these five financial priorities. In keeping with Ron Blue's testimony, we believe that being disciplined about the use of money is important at any income level. Tithing and giving decisions are the topic of a whole other book; suffice it to say here that that the decision to give generously and from the heart is of the utmost importance for the Christ follower. Patrick Johnson, vice president of Generous Giving, writes, "Giving enables the Western church to break free of the bonds of materialism and to invest in the advance of the kingdom of God." Our house's Second Story relates to all the various aspects of our money outflow.

His master said to him, "Well done, good and faithful servant. You have been faithful over a little; I will set you over much. Enter into the joy of your master."

MATTHEW 25:21, ESV

A person of faith ought to be guided by some kind of aligning principles in the ways he or she earns, saves, and invests money to meet future needs. Our stewardship house's *Third Story* addresses the ways by which we procure wealth—our money inflow. It is built from the principles that guide any of our income-producing pursuits and, for this book's purpose, particularly how we make saving and investment decisions that match up with our values.

One important aspect of stewardship on the Third Story is planning. In business, great leaders and managers always make provisions for the future. Whether it is in the form of emergency reserves, contingency plans, or research and development, planning for the future is an essential part of good management. Proverbs 6 drives this lesson home: "Go to the ant, O sluggard; consider her ways and be wise. Without having any chief, officer or ruler, [the ant] prepares her bread in summer and gathers her food in harvest" (verses 6–8, ESV). Even insects have better planning skills than many human stewards.

> Seven years of great abundance are coming throughout the land of Egypt, but seven years of famine will follow them. Then all the abundance in Egypt will be forgotten, and the famine will ravage the land.

> GENESIS 41:29–30

In Genesis, Joseph counseled Pharaoh about how to use wisely the abundant crops Egypt had harvested. Most of us will never have the benefit of receiving prophetic dream interpretations as Joseph did, but we can still glean wisdom from his story. Economies work in cycles, like the seasons in nature. Spring and summer always come after winter; that's the hopeful news for people and companies during bleak financial times. But also, winter always comes after summer and fall—a warning to those who revel in the fruit of fair weather.

The key is to be prepared for the changing seasons. As managers of God's resources, we individual stewards must make future provision for ourselves, our family, and others. Consider Paul's words: "If anyone does not provide for his relatives, and especially for members of his household, he has denied the faith and is worse than an unbeliever" (1 Timothy 5:8, ESV). Worse than an unbeliever? That is pretty strong language, even for the apostle Paul. Context is important here: some of the religious leaders of Paul's day were making a show of giving generously to the temple while their widowed mothers were starving in poverty. The moral of the story? It is absolutely biblical to think about the long-term needs of your family.

Once we understand our relationship to God and the greatest commandments (the First Story), and once we begin consecrating our decisions about lifestyle and giving to the Lord as part of our integral daily faith (the Second Story), the next natural step in the progression is to ask, *How do I prepare for the future needs of my family?* In the Three-Story House analogy, the question to ask on the Third Story is, *Are my investment choices to work toward those future needs reflecting my values?*

WHY DOES IT MATTER?

Better a little with righteousness than much gain with injustice.

PROVERBS 16:8

The Lord's Prayer begins, "Our Father in heaven, hallowed be your name" (Matthew 6:9). I once heard a whole sermon that focused on this one phrase: "Hallowed be your name." Hallowed is not a word commonly used in the English language.

The definition according to *Merriam-Webster's Dictionary* is "made holy or set apart as holy." BRI represents an opportunity to *set apart* the resources entrusted to us by aligning our investments with our faith values. It is not a legalistic requirement, but rather a free response and a reflection of our love for God and for others. For committed Christians, BRI is a natural extension of our vital act of daily worship.

The Three Stories in this analogy all come together to form a unified structure—a house with interconnecting rooms. Part of our faith journey as Christ followers is the process of striving to morally and biblically align our behavior (First Story), our spending decisions (Second Story), and our investment and earnings decisions (Third Story). The Three Stories are not in this order because one is more important than another; rather, they must be naturally considered and mastered in this order.

For example, in order to have funds available for stewardship decisions about saving and investment, we must first gain control of biblical stewardship in the areas of spending, giving, and lifestyle. And unless we first strive to love the Lord and to love others in our daily walk, we probably won't care about how we spend money or give to others. All of these decisions are rooted in the attitude and character of the heart, and we must walk through one Story before we can proceed to the next.

> Jesus said, "If you are offering your gift at the altar and there remember that your brother has something against you, leave your gift there before the altar and go. First be reconciled to your brother, and then come and offer your gift."
>
> MATTHEW 5:23–24, ESV

When all Three Stories are aligned to biblical values, the

house stands straight. When they are somewhat misaligned, the house will lean a little. If they are too far out of alignment, gravity will bring the house down with a crash. It's important to note that this is true of both our financial and spiritual-moral lives; the two are intertwined in the universe God has designed. If our spiritual and moral lives are totally out of alignment, everything can come crashing down.

Moses warned about alignment "drift." Immediately after coming down from Mount Sinai and giving the people of Israel the Ten Commandments, Moses said, "Be careful to do what the LORD your God has commanded you; do not turn aside to the right or to the left. Walk in obedience to all that the LORD your God has commanded you, so that you may live and prosper and prolong your days in the land that you will possess" (Deuteronomy 5:32–33). Joshua, before leading Israel across the Jordan River, repeated Moses' warning to the people: "Be careful to obey all the law my servant Moses gave you; do not turn from it to the right or left" (Joshua 1:7).

As fallen creatures, we are in need of constant and repeated spiritual alignment. If we pursue God and His kingdom values, we will see measurable, significant growth in our hearts and habits. But we're never going to be perfect in this life, and don't be surprised to see progress in one area while discovering neglect in another. For example, you might be reading the Bible and demonstrating love toward your neighbor, while feeding an impulsive spending habit that's dragging your family down with financial worry. Or you might be helping a homeless stranger, but neglecting a family member who needs your forgiveness. We are all flawed human beings and everyone has his or her blind spots. Honoring God with our investments is part of this life-in-progress, and no one should expect to get it perfectly the first time out. Or the second. Or the third… But you can expect to learn and grow.

If you regret your prior money-handling decisions, consider John Newton, who in 1772 wrote the famous poem-turned-hymn "Amazing Grace." Newton was a former slave trader who, upon his conversion, became one of the great abolitionists of eighteenth-century England. His personal story brings new meaning to the line, "I once was lost, but now am found, was blind but now I see." The facts of his past, which he could never change, didn't keep him from living a powerful, God-honoring life going forward. Once we experience a change of heart, there is good news! We serve a God of second chances. Everything in our lives—including the parts we wish we had done differently—become part of the journey in which God uses situations, people, and the living Word to instruct us and to open our eyes to new opportunities, as we strive to be more like Him.

BRI is not some legalistic requirement to help us feel more righteous. The Pharisees were experts in this kind of thinking and Jesus lambasted them for it. In the early church a faction of Jewish believers went around teaching that the physical ritual of circumcision—carried over from God's Old Covenant with Israel—was a necessary requirement for Gentiles to have a relationship with God. Paul put an end to this debate in his letter to the Romans, arguing that faith alone was sufficient. In Paul's words, "Circumcision is a matter of the heart, by the Spirit, not by the letter [of the law]" (Romans 2:29, ESV).

It is the grace of God and the blood of Christ alone that delivers us from ourselves. BRI is not a guilt decision; it is a heart decision. Looking back, it's an expression of joy and gratitude for the work God has already done in us. Looking forward, it's an opportunity for alignment with the other areas of our life where we are already actively seeking to honor the Lord.

It is also important to note early in this book that deciding *when* and *why* to invest are just as important as choosing *where* to invest. For example, when is investing good stewardship and when is it selfish? What is the difference between investing and hoarding? If we are not investing for the right reasons, then it doesn't really matter whether we're investing in biblically "pure" investments; a selfish motivation can make any investment pursuit impure for the investor.

In his book, *Master Your Money,* Ron Blue explains one way to determine the extent to which a family's investments should go, without going too far. He talks about drawing "finish lines," where each family determines for themselves "how much is enough" to accumulate in order to meet their unique, predetermined lifestyle needs.[7] Whatever resources God chooses to bless us with above and beyond the finish line may then be freed up for other purposes, such as generous giving for eternal impact. For purposes of this book we will assume that you have already drawn your own finish lines, defining how much is enough to save and invest for your current needs and future goals. If you have not yet gone through that process, perhaps you will discover and refine them while you are learning about BRI.

Countless other books and sermons have been devoted to the principles described in the Foundation and the First and Second Stories of this stewardship house we are building; we will touch on them again only briefly in the next few pages in order to be sure that the Third Story—the primary topic of this book—will be based on the prior, well-established levels. In the Appendix, I've included a reading list of other books and websites to consider if you'd like to learn more about the First and Second Stories of the House.

Building on this imagery of a Three-Story House, let us continue exploring what it means to invest with integrity.

1. LAYING THE FOUNDATION

> "Everyone then who hears these words of mine and
> does them will be like a wise man who built his house
> on the rock. And the rain fell, and the floods came, and
> the winds blew and beat on that house, but it did not
> fall, because it had been founded on the rock."
>
> MATTHEW 7:24–25, ESV

When discussing biblical stewardship and the Three-Story
House analogy, our Foundation is built on what we hold to be
true about God and the Bible. In every masonry foundation, the
cornerstone is the first stone set in the construction of the foundation. It is important because all other stones will be set in reference to this stone. Paul uses the terminology of a homebuilder
in describing Jesus in his letter to Ephesus: "You are…members
of [God's] household, built on the foundation of the apostles
and prophets, with Christ Jesus himself as the *chief cornerstone*"
(Ephesians 2:19–20, emphasis added). Jesus Christ is the reference point for everything else that we believe and practice. Our
doctrinal Foundation includes many other "stones," but for purposes of this book I will focus on three of them—three central
biblical themes—that help form the Foundation of our Three-
Story House of stewardship:

GOD OWNS IT ALL

> The earth is the LORD's, and everything in it, the world,
> and all who live in it; for he founded it upon the seas
> and established it upon the waters.
>
> PSALM 24:1–2

In the book of Genesis, God gave humankind dominion, but

not ultimate ownership, over all the earth (1:28). Therefore we are His stewards. Other words for steward are trustee or manager. *Merriam-Webster's Dictionary* defines stewardship as "the careful and responsible management of something entrusted to one's care." In a company, managers don't own the employees, but neither do they let employees run wild. Human capital is cultivated, instructed, and organized in order to accomplish the objectives of the owners (or shareholders)—namely, to bring a valuable product or service to the marketplace and earn a return on investment. In the same way, God blesses us with responsibility for His resources, with an expectation that we will use them to accomplish His purposes, which are eternal.

God's Perspective Is Eternal

> Have you not known? Have you not heard? The LORD is the everlasting God, the Creator of the ends of the earth. He does not faint or grow weary; his understanding is unsearchable.

Isaiah 40:28, esv

God expects our stewardship to have eternal implications. In his book *The Treasure Principle,* Randy Alcorn gives an illustration of what eternal perspective really looks like. Imagine a white board that has a line drawn all the way across the board with arrows extending into infinity both ways. This line represents all of eternity. Now take a really fine-tip marker and make a tiny little dot on the line.

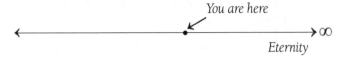

You are here

Eternity

This dot represents your life on earth. Talk about feeling

insignificant. In the vast stretches of eternity, one hundred years is a blip on the screen. We are reminded of this in James 4:14: "Why, you do not even know what will happen tomorrow. What is your life? You are a mist that appears for a little while and then vanishes." One of the principles in Alcorn's book is that we as Christians should "live for the line, not the dot." For a season, we are stewards of all God has created. Then we return to dust and the next generation of stewards carries on. That's why it's so important to use this limited number of years as effectively as possible, managing the resources and opportunities in our hands to make a difference in our world and ultimately to have an eternal impact.

God Is Provider and Protector

> "And who of you by being worried can add a single hour to his life? And why are you worried about clothing? Observe how the lilies of the field grow; they do not toil nor do they spin, yet I say to you that not even Solomon in all his glory clothed himself like one of these."
>
> MATTHEW 6:27–29, NASB

God promises to provide for our every human need. Our nature, of course, is to blur the line between what we truly need, and what we think we want out of life. To compound matters, so many things are out of our control that if we focused on all the unpredictable factors that could disrupt our life plans, we would probably go crazy. Remember Jesus' parable of the fool who, as a result of a successful harvest, had such an abundance he had nowhere to store it all. "Then he said, 'This is what I'll do. I will tear down my barns and build bigger ones, and there I will store my surplus grain. And I'll say to myself, "You have plenty of grain laid up for many years. Take life easy; eat, drink and be merry.'" But God said to him, 'You fool! This very night your life will be demanded from you. Then who will get what you have prepared for yourself?'" (Luke 12:18–20). There is nothing wrong with making provision for the future, but placing our trust in our barns instead of in God can distract from our relationship with God and lead to anxiety. This bit of foundational wisdom may sound odd coming from a financial advisor, whose job is to help others make plans for the future. To be clear, making plans is an important element of good stewardship. In fact, God also gave us the gift of imagination so that we might dream big. No matter how elaborate our plans, however, ultimately we are called to place our trust in the Lord for His provision and protection.

At my company we implement state-of-the-art software that can model out advanced planning scenarios based on certain assumptions such as inflation, market returns, and taxes. One of the features of the software is the ability to "stress-test" different investment strategies to see how they might hold up in case of a major market crash. As you might imagine, after the Great Recession of 2008–2009, that scenario has garnered a lot more attention.

In the institutional world, this process is called a Monte Carlo Analysis.[*] Every time I mention that to clients I get the same response: "Monte Carlo? Sounds like gambling to me!" In truth, it's a complex formula that takes into account all of the stock market's historical returns and wild swings, then crunches

---

[*]Assumed rates of return and standard deviation assumptions used in the Monte Carlo analysis are based on historical return data for the benchmark index for the asset class. Past performance is no guarantee of future results. Results may vary with each use and over time.

IMPORTANT: The projections or other information generated by Monte Carlo Analysis regarding the likelihood of various investment outcomes are hypothetical in nature, do not reflect actual investment results and are not guarantees of future results.

the numbers a thousand different ways to generate random samples of hypothetical returns. If you think back to Statistics 101 in college, the Monte Carlo creates a bell curve, or statistical probability, of success. In this case, we define success as not running out of money!

Whenever I do this analysis, I always aim to design financial strategies having around 80-percent or better probability of success. Sometimes clients ask, "Why not aim for 100 percent?" The answer is simple: the future is unknown, and while we can reasonably plan for the future, many factors are out of our control. Inflation could run rampant, a war could break out in another part of the world, or the rules for Social Security could change. The list goes on. Even today's best forecasting technology cannot predict the future.

The Old Testament Proverb says it this way, "In his heart a man plans his course, but the LORD determines his steps" (Proverbs 16:9). E.G. "Jay" Link, author of *To Whom Much Is Given* and founder of Stewardship Ministries, once said, "Our trust must always be set on the provider, not the provision." Ultimately, God is our provider and protector.

> Yours, O LORD, is the greatness, the power, the glory, the victory, and the majesty. Everything in the heavens and on earth is yours, O LORD, and this is your kingdom. We adore you as the one who is over all things. Wealth and honor come from you alone, for you rule over everything. Power and might are in your hand, and at your discretion people are made great and given strength.

> 1 CHRONICLES 29:11-12, NLT

2. A JOURNEY OF DISCOVERY

> Many people measure their success by wealth, recognition, power, and status. There's nothing wrong with those, but if that's all you're focused on, you're missing the boat.... Using your time and talent to serve others—that's when truly meaningful success can come your way.[8]
>
> KEN BLANCHARD

As I share my personal story, my hope is that you are encouraged to explore the opportunity that BRI offers to align faith and investment decisions, just as my own process of discovery encouraged me. Come along on this journey with me and see if you identify with all or part of my story.

FAITH JOURNEY—MY FOUNDATION AND FIRST STORY

Growing up, I did not consider myself a religious person. My father's side of the family celebrates a Jewish heritage, although Dad was never very religious in the formal sense. My mother's side of the family has English Protestant and some Catholic roots but was mostly agnostic when I was young, giving deference to the idea that God exists but not interested in organized religion. I was young when my parents divorced, and matters of faith were generally not discussed at home, other than to encourage me to explore for myself what I might choose to believe. So my views on success and life purpose were shaped largely by mainstream secular American culture. I assumed that there is a success track to life, and the key to happiness is getting into college, finding a good job, and moving up the social ladder.

Another important part of my worldview was shaped by my dad's success in business. Dad prospered as an industrial engineer and business owner. His engineering firm employed over one hundred professionals and contracted with major aircraft and aerospace companies in the United States. His firm built industrial research facilities for such purposes as testing advanced concepts in aerodynamics, developing jet propulsion in high atmosphere, and rocket engine testing for use in space. I sometimes joke that providing financial planning and investment services is not rocket science, but it runs in the family!

My dad was also a talented pilot, and the year I was born (1977) he purchased his own private jet, a Cessna Citation I, for the company. It was the only private jet aircraft that could be flown by one pilot, and Dad flew it himself. My dad's career accomplishments were truly remarkable and reinforced my impression of the path to success. I feel fortunate to enjoy close relationships with both of my parents, and over the years I observed that money didn't necessarily bring happiness or make life any easier. In fact, I realized just the opposite—that "success" could sometimes make life more complicated. Nonetheless, without an alternate worldview I held tightly to my definition of success leading up to college.

Earning a spot at UCLA was the first major achievement on my ladder of success, and I immediately joined a social fraternity to celebrate this accomplishment. But the buzz only lasted so long, and one day I was struck with an epiphany. I imagined the future and saw an endless cycle of accomplishments and diminishing returns, spinning perpetually like a caged hamster's wheel. I also realized that the world's definition of success was fickle. People work hard to build castles in the sand, only to see them swept away by circumstances beyond their control. That's when God began tugging at my heart, leading me to question the meaning of my existence.

While investigating the world's great religions in search of answers, I stumbled across a paperback Bible and started reading it. There was something attractive about the teachings of Christianity that rang true in my heart. Soon afterward, through a series of events and people who came into my life, I came to understand some of the Bible's central themes—that I was separated from God by my sin, that no matter how hard I tried I could never live up to the standard of perfect obedience God required, and that through relationship with Jesus Christ—who paid the penalty for my sins—I could have eternal life in a personal relationship with God. In January 1996, as a freshman at UCLA, I gave my life to Christ by accepting Him into my heart as Lord and Savior. At that moment, I experienced an incredible sense of peace and purpose.

From there, God kept bringing mentors and leaders into my life who helped me grow in the Word and equipped me to serve in Greek Life, an outreach ministry of Campus Crusade for Christ (now "Cru") to fraternities and sororities. After graduating from UCLA, I started work as a public accountant and seemed to get break after break…

Fast-forward ten years: I felt incredibly blessed. I was married to the love of my life, we each had great jobs, and by maintaining a modest lifestyle renting a small apartment, we had become diligent savers. Throughout our marriage we also tithed faithfully, and even discovered a joy in giving, as we began to see the positive impact of our gifts to local ministries. Don't get me wrong; we certainly made our share of mistakes along the way, and life was not perfect. The important thing for us was that we were not treading the meaningless hamster wheel, grabbing for what the world called "success." Rather, we kept an open-hand attitude, understanding that God gives and God takes away, blessed be His name.

I didn't realize it at the time, but the Lord had provided a solid Foundation for my stewardship House. My First Story (relationships) had been framed out with the help of key spiritual mentors in my life and by learning how to be a good husband in marriage, but it was still a work in progress. I wasn't aware of the Second Story (wealth outflow) beyond the importance of tithing, but in what I knew, I was honoring God. And I had no idea that stewardship had anything to do with a Third Story (wealth inflow); I defaulted to the method I'd learned growing up: work diligently and honestly, and earn more money.

Then came the test.

CAREER JOURNEY

God allowed me to taste a preview of my old definition of success early in my career as a young vice president of an investment firm that was experiencing tremendous growth. It was an opportunity that promised a bright financial future. But seven years into my career, I felt God asking me, *Are you willing to give this up?* For a long time we had felt a tug to move back to Spokane, Washington, where my wife had been born and raised. After a lot of prayer we trusted God and made a choice to step out of the fast lane. In the fall of 2007, we both left high-paying jobs in Los Angeles and moved to Spokane.

Looking back, it was one of the best decisions we have made. Spokane is a beautiful place and we love it here. At the time, however, it was much harder to walk away from the opportunities in Los Angeles than I thought it would be. Once we settled in Spokane, I believed that my CPA background, financial training, and past experience with institutional money management made me uniquely qualified to serve families in an advisor role. So with the help of several mentors and a few loyal clients I started an independent practice in January 2008.

If anyone were to ask me what business to start at the cusp

of a financial meltdown and the ensuing Great Recession that followed, my answer would not have been a financial services firm. After all, 2008 was the year Lehman Brothers* went bankrupt, Bear Stearns* collapsed, and Merrill Lynch* was rescued by Bank of America*. Not to mention the stock market crash, which registered a loss of -53.9 percent as measured by the S&P 500 Index† from January 2008 to the March 2009 lows.[9] Navigating the second-steepest bear market in US history—second only to the Great Depression of the 1930s—is definitely not how I would recommend starting out a financial services practice.

But God is faithful. Years later, I learned that my former employer in Los Angeles ran into serious legal trouble and filed for bankruptcy protection. It's interesting how time lends perspective. When faced with a crossroads in life, we might feel at the time that we are making bold spiritual moves and great sacrifices. But as history unfolds, so often we find out later that it wasn't about us at all. Rather, God was protecting us from something we couldn't see around the corner.

DISCOVERING THE SECOND STORY

When I first launched my practice, I did not have a faith-based approach to serving clients. Yet within six months of opening our doors the practice took an interesting turn. My wife and I signed up for Howard Dayton's ten-week *Crown Financial Bible*

---

*Any reference to Lehman Brothers, Bear Stearns, Merrill Lynch, and Bank of America is for illustrative purposes only in connection to historical, factual events and does not constitute a recommendation to buy or sell any security. See also important disclosures.
† The Standard & Poor's 500 Index (S&P 500) is a capitalization weighted index of 500 stocks designed to measure performance of the broad domestic economy through changes in the aggregate market value of 500 stocks representing all major industries. The S&P 500 is an unmanaged index which cannot be invested into directly. Past performance is no guarantee of future results. All indexes are unmanaged and cannot be invested into directly. Past performance is no guarantee of future results.

Study (now published by Compass as *Navigating Your Finances God's Way™*).[10] It was a total paradigm shift to realize just how much God has to say about finances. For example, did you know there are over 2300 verses in the Bible about money and possessions?[11] That's more than four times the number of verses found in Scripture on other important topics, such as faith or prayer. The Bible study gave us a complete tour of the Second Story of stewardship—solid biblical teaching on subjects such as avoiding debt, giving generously (beyond the tithe, or 10 percent), and counting the cost before taking on risk.

After we completed the study, my wife and I decided to make significant changes to get our personal financial house in order. As we were going through that process, I remember thinking to myself, *I bet other families could avoid financial ruin by hearing about biblical financial principles*. Around that time, a close friend introduced me to Kingdom Advisors, a teaching and equipping ministry dedicated to helping financial advisors implement biblical financial principles with clients. Founded by Ron Blue, former president of Ronald Blue and Company, Kingdom Advisors was originally the vision of Larry Burkett (1939–2003). Ron and Larry were longtime friends and co-laborers in Christ, serving together on a number of boards, including Crown Financial Ministries. Ron shared the story of how Larry asked him to carry the torch and to start this amazing ministry shortly before he passed away. Ron was faithful to that calling.

TWO PATHS CONVERGE: FAITH AND CAREER

In the summer of 2009, as the stock market crumbled around me and headlines in the *Wall Street Journal* insinuated the End of the World had come, I became a member of Kingdom Advisors and completed the Qualified Kingdom Advisor™ training.

During the same period I also found incredible peace in a book authored by Ron Blue and Jeremy White, *Surviving Financial Meltdown,* which wisely counsels to turn down "the noise" and turn up God's Word in times of economic uncertainty. That book was so powerful, I bought a case in bulk and distributed them among clients and friends. The training and new resources I discovered had a deeply profound impact on me, transforming my secular wealth-management practice into a marketplace ministry. It was as though two paths were converging in my life, combining on the one side my Christian faith and newly discovered biblical financial principles, and on the other side my secular career training and experience in finance and institutional money management.

Looking back, I can see that God had a plan. My encounter with God and my ministry experiences in college, combined with years of specialized business experience in the financial industry, had prepared me to teach biblical financial principles in a professional setting and to help other families along their stewardship journey. I wish I could say I planned it that way, that I had it all figured out. The truth is, the transformation in my practice would not have been possible if not for Kingdom Advisors. This organization has provided the cornerstone of my company's service model for delivering biblical financial wisdom to our clients—especially to those who have been blessed with abundance and are looking to advance "from success to significance" (borrowing a phrase from Lloyd Reeb's book of the same title).[12]

> In your own life, have you considered how your faith journey and career training might converge into a marketplace ministry within your own spheres of influence?

Discovering the Third Story: 4800 Miles of Due Diligence

> Do not follow where the path may lead. Go instead
> where there is no path and leave a trail.
>
> Ralph Waldo Emerson

As I continued to explore what the Bible had to say about finance, I received an invitation to attend a seminar about BRI in Seattle. It was the first time I had heard the term BRI specifically, and all I really knew was that it had something to do with applying faith to investment decisions. I wanted to investigate further. After attending the seminar, I felt as if I had discovered a whole Third Story of the house that I had yet to explore.

In February 2010, I traveled to Atlanta for the annual Kingdom Advisor conference, where I joined hundreds of other financial advisors committed to providing professional advice from a Christian worldview. It was the first professional conference I had ever attended where each teaching session was preceded with live worship. It was awe-inspiring. For me, the conference was the turning point in my journey.

While the number of advisors who implement BRI represents just a small community within Kingdom Advisors, in practice BRI has always resonated strongly with the Kingdom Advisors philosophy. Take, as evidence of this, the conference's chosen venue. Kingdom Advisors chose the Omni Hotel because Omni Hotels decline to offer pornographic content in the rooms. Most all of the major chains do offer porn, because it is so profitable. As a result, it was a unique challenge for Kingdom Advisors to find a morally safe hotel that could accommodate hundreds of Christian financial advisors.

In fact, did you know that hotel porn is so lucrative that when a new hotel is built, often the providers of porn content will purchase and install the TV equipment for all the rooms at no charge to the hotel, simply in exchange for the exclusive rights to provide "adult" pay-per-view content? For the Omni to say "no, thank you" to porn probably cost them millions of dollars in electronics equipment. And yet the Omni manages to be one of the few profitable hotel chains. Why? I believe that God honors those who honor Him. This doesn't imply that BRI will outperform. We address that later in Chapter 5, "Myth-Busting." But it does serve as an example of living our faith with integrity in all aspects of life, including business.

At the conference, I had the privilege of personally meeting many of the investment managers and national leaders who were blazing a trail for BRI, including Ron Blue. Although BRI was still a relatively new idea in Christian financial circles, and practically unheard of on Wall Street, on the flight home I felt God calling me to learn more about BRI.

The following year, Kingdom Advisors membership had grown so large that the Omni in Atlanta could not accommodate all of the conference participants. Instead of choosing a larger hotel in the Atlanta area, Kingdom Advisors decided to honor the Omni's commitment to family values and moved the entire conference to the Omni Orlando at ChampionsGate. In keeping with tradition, every session of the conference opened with live worship. Except this time, twice the number of Kingdom Advisors were joining in. God is definitely up to something here.

When BRI first emerged as a mutual fund choice over fifteen years ago, it was called many things, including Morally Responsible Investing, Faith-Based Investing, or simply Ethical Investing. The phrase "Biblically Responsible Investing" is believed to have been first coined by Dan Hardt, of Dan Hardt Financial Services in Louisville, Kentucky, sometime in 2004. We will discuss the history of BRI and capital markets in more detail in Chapter 6.

We want to be moral, yes. But the word 'moral' means so many different things to different people, that it doesn't really describe the source of truth. Morality is not the source of Truth, nor are societal norms. The Bible is the source of Truth. The Bible defines morality and everything else....We just wanted a phrase that went back to the source.

Dan Hardt

I have enjoyed getting to know Dan and learning about his story. When I asked how Dan first learned about BRI, his experience sounded very similar to my own. He said, "I had never given any thought at all to the moral side of where money was being invested." Then in the mid-90s, Dan got a phone call from Art Ally, president of The Timothy Plan[5] mutual funds. Dan said, "I don't know where he got my name, but I listened politely. I had never heard of him before, nor had I ever heard of the concept before." At the time, Dan shared honestly that he was not keen on adding yet another variable to the existing complexities of picking out the right funds for somebody.

So while the BRI concept made somewhat of an impression on Dan, he didn't do anything about it. It took him some years before he came to believe that some people might want this type of screening. The turning point in Dan's story came when a lady approached him for help with her investments. Dan told her

*Any reference to the Timothy Plan mutual funds is for illustrative purposes only in connection to historical, factual events and does not constitute an offer to buy or sell any security. Investing in any mutual fund involves risk, including possible loss of principal. For social, moral, and faith-based funds, returns may be lower than if the investor made decisions based solely on other investment considerations, but they could also be higher. Investors should consider the investment objectives, risks, charges, and expenses of the investment company carefully before investing. The prospectus and, if available, the summary prospectus contain this and other important information about the investment company.

about screened investing, as he had started to do with all his clients, and let her decide whether she wanted screening or not. The problem was, she couldn't decide. She said to Dan, "Well, when I work with my boss and we get stuck, he always asks me, 'What is the right thing to do?'" So she asked Dan the same question: "What is the right thing to do?"

It hit him like a ton of bricks, because the right thing was obvious to him, and he realized he had been dancing around it for several years. Dan said, "It was at that point that I got serious about BRI." He reflected how BRI has not yet reached a tipping point. "It's very easy for a practitioner to hear about BRI, as I did in the mid-90s, and sort of put it on the back shelf for a very long time. And they may or may not ever come around." Dan continued, "I happened to be surrounded by other people—whom I liked for many reasons—who were also advocates of moral screening. Other folks don't necessarily have circles like that."

Dan's nonconfrontational style drew him into a position of leadership within the BRI community group of Kingdom Advisors, which he led for six years or so. Dan shared that, unfortunately, in the area of investing from a Christian perspective, there are some who dismiss all this screening as silliness, and others who are adamant that if you don't screen you're a sinner. For a topic that a lot of people have never even heard of, there's a lot of polarization among Christian financial advisors. Of course, differences in theology, thought, and opinion are certainly nothing new in the history of the Christian faith.

Dan has helped bridge those differences in a spirit of love and humility, wanting to figure out the best way forward in being biblical in everything we do. What BRI has been able to establish is a "big tent" approach where evangelical Christian believers across many denominations and traditions are able to find common ground on key issues. We will cover more about BRI's big-tent approach later in the book.

Dan's story is like so many other stories I have encountered along the way, including my own. In the midst of conducting business as usual, someone or something triggers a turning point where suddenly BRI matters.

Déjà Vu: A New/Old Concept

Looking back, my first introduction to BRI was actually over eight years ago in 2005, when I was working for a large institutional money manager. The firm had recently been hired to manage a prominent Catholic foundation, and the foundation's investment policy required that it exclude certain industries, such as abortion and alcohol. The abortion restriction was easy because at the time it so happened that the firm's research team did not have any pharmaceutical companies in the portfolio. But the portfolio manager did hold investments in a large alcohol company. I remember that triggered some heated debate. At the time, I thought to myself, *What's the big deal?* After all, at the time the maker of alcoholic beverages was expanding rapidly in China, and Warren Buffet had famously taken a big stake in the company.

As it later turned out, the company was indeed a great investment. That particular stock doubled in a comparatively short period of time. Considering that portfolio managers live and die by performance, it's understandable why the manager would argue to keep the alcohol stock in the portfolio. Ultimately, the Catholic foundation got their wish to create a custom portfolio that excluded alcohol from their holdings, perhaps because the portfolio manager did not want to lose a twenty-million-dollar account. Historically, however, the average investor does not wield that kind of influence. Interestingly, the performance of the custom portfolio was not all that different compared to other clients, as the alcohol position represented only around 3 percent of the manager's strategy. There were plenty of other good investment ideas in the portfolio that also did well, and the Catholic foundation owned proportionately more of those other investments.

That's how I think BRI has achieved a foothold in most cases to date. A large institutional client makes a custom request, Wall Street acquiesces, and statistically one sees very little change in performance. So what about Main Street investors? How do they influence portfolio managers to exclude investment in companies that conflict with their values?

THE VICE FUND*

To understand an abstract concept, sometimes it is helpful to think in terms of opposites. Another turning point that helped shape my view about BRI was a tax and estate-planning conference in Las Vegas I attended about six years ago, hosted by the American Institute of Certified Public Accountants. What could be more dangerous than turning loose a bunch of accountants in Las Vegas, right? My wife came with me and we actually had a nice time staying at the Bellagio hotel.

Since many of the conference topics pertained to investments for high-net-worth families, several of the conference sponsors were investment companies. As anyone who has ever attended a work conference will attest, these events are intentionally structured around breaks and receptions, in order to herd all the participants toward the sponsor booths. One booth in particular drew my curiosity. In big letters draped over the

---

*Any reference to the Vice Fund is for illustrative purposes only in connection to historical, factual events and does not constitute an offer to buy or sell any security. Investing in any mutual fund involves risk, including possible loss of principal.

booth it said, "The Vice Fund." So I stopped by on my way to the coffee stand as I went for my pre-mid-afternoon caffeine fix (irony intended). The booth representative was a young college grad, wearing a nice suit and tie and eager to talk to somebody.

"What's this?" I asked.

He replied in a matter-of-fact way, "Oh, we're the Vice Fund." The perplexed look on my face must have encouraged him to continue explaining; he picked up some brochures from the table. "We are a mutual fund that only invests in products that are addictive, because we believe people will keep buying them during both up and down economies."

I scratched my head and continued in polite conversation. "So what kind of companies do you invest in?"

He said, "Well, primarily defense, alcohol, tobacco, and gaming companies."

I thanked him for his time and went on my way. At the time I knew nothing about BRI, but learning about the Vice Fund did give me something to think about. Shaking my head in mild amusement, I said to myself, *Well, at least they picked the right city to set up shop!*

An Evolving Process

Over the past decade, dozens of investment companies and mutual funds have sprung up offering BRI portfolios to align with Christian values. As a result, a talent pool has emerged offering some pretty solid funds. But the purpose of this book is not to share with you the "Five Hottest BRI Mutual Funds." We would encourage you to work with a competent financial advisor who can help you implement a strategy that fits into the bigger picture as you pursue your other stewardship goals and objectives.

For many years Ron Blue was neutral on the BRI approach,

largely because of the lack of options available among the managers. Over the years, as access to quality managers has improved and the talent pool of informed financial advisors has expanded, Ron's perspective has evolved as well. He now openly endorses BRI as a valid approach and a personal decision that each family needs to make. The purpose of BRI is not to shame or guilt Christians into thinking and investing this way. By no means! Remember, it was the Pharisees—the self-righteous "religious people"—with whom Jesus dealt most harshly in His teachings.

Rather, BRI is an opportunity to extend our vital act of worship to include the process of saving and investing for future needs and goals. The call to action in this book is to search the Scriptures for yourself, pray about it, talk with your pastor and financial advisor about it, and be faithful to what God is teaching you in this area.

> There are three conversions necessary: the conversion
> of the heart, mind, and purse.
>
> MARTIN LUTHER[13]

What I have learned from other advisors committed to BRI is that embracing the BRI concept is a process. Personally, it took me over a year to get fully comfortable with implementing BRI with clients, and I am not alone. Dan Hardt shared that it took him several years from the time he was first introduced to the concept to the point that he fully embraced it. As I mentioned, embracing the BRI concept was a process for Ron Blue as well. Financial advisors who have a strong Christian faith and a genuine desire to honor God in every area of life seem to follow a natural progression in warming up to BRI.

First, advisors take an initial interest in BRI, but don't implement it—either because they're too busy or too skeptical. Then they encounter some turning point and realize the industry has evolved to the point where BRI can be implemented without sacrificing high standards of excellence. Finally, they experience a heart change, believing that BRI is worth communicating and offering to their clients.

> I am not ashamed of the gospel, because it is the power
> of God for the salvation of everyone who believes: first
> for the Jew, then for the Gentile.

ROMANS 1:16

Embracing BRI and the opportunity to align investment decisions with faith is a process. I hope my story provides a fresh perspective and that this book serves as a resource, not only for the church and the investing public, but also for other financial advisors to communicate with their clients and firms about the opportunity BRI presents for spiritual alignment.

3. HOW BRI WORKS

When your values are clear, your decisions are easy.

ROY DISNEY (WALT'S BROTHER)

To help understand how the BRI screening process works, we will use the analogy of an employer interviewing job candidates. For the sake of illustration, let's say the opening is for a kindergarten teaching position. Beyond confirming the proper teaching credentials, the employer will check each candidate against a list of characteristics that make for a great kindergarten teacher, such as a love of kids, patience, and empathy. With these specific criteria in mind, the school principal will go about interviewing job candidates to find a good match. Once a qualified candidate has been identified, what is the last step an employer typically performs before making a hiring decision? A background check, of course! Every employer in America runs a background check to make sure no criminal records exist to disqualify a candidate.

For an investment fund manager, BRI screening works in much the same way as a background check works for an employer. The fund managers know what criteria make for a great investment idea, financially speaking. For example, they might be looking for companies that offer a new product or service, a strong management team, a healthy balance sheet, prospects for growth, or an undervalued stock price. Once they find a viable "candidate," BRI fund managers can now also run a "background check" against BRI databases that track corporate activity and SEC filings to make sure the investment idea (for example, a corporate stock or bond) doesn't trigger any moral red flags by biblical standards.

HERE'S A VISUAL OF HOW IT WORKS:

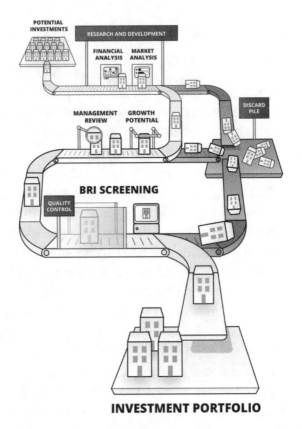

POTENTIAL INVESTMENTS

RESEARCH AND DEVELOPMENT

FINANCIAL ANALYSIS MARKET ANALYSIS

DISCARD PILE

MANAGEMENT REVIEW GROWTH POTENTIAL

BRI SCREENING

QUALITY CONTROL

INVESTMENT PORTFOLIO

Fund managers who implement BRI are looking for great investments, just like any other investment manager. The difference is simply that BRI fund managers add an extra layer of due diligence to their research process by running moral "background checks"—that is, using BRI databases to screen for moral issues. We'll discuss in greater detail in the next chapter the ways to define what's moral and what's not.

It's important to note that fund managers who do not screen are not necessarily looking for immoral companies; the moral implications simply do not register on their radar screens. For that reason, I refer to non-screened funds as "values-neutral." Without an intentional evaluation system in place, the likelihood of a mutual fund owning companies that fail the BRI screens is merely a game of statistics. The larger the mutual fund's size, the greater the number of its individual holdings, and therefore the greater the chances that it owns companies that fail the BRI screens…and the more such companies it is likely to own. BRI presents an opportunity to install a filtering system into the investment process that allows fund managers to be more intentional about what types of companies make it into the portfolio.

In 2010 I had lunch with a gentleman who serves in an upper-management role for a large, publicly traded timber company. Intrigued by the BRI concept, he asked if his own employer was on the BRI-screened list. As a favor, I called one of the BRI fund managers we worked with at the time and ran the company through the BRI database. The company passed with flying colors and even received positive marks for environmental sustainability with regard to its harvesting techniques. Needless to say, this individual was relieved to hear the news. I think all of us would desire to work for a company that we believe is doing more good in the world than harm. BRI offers an opportunity for investors to put their money to work in this same kind of company.

How to Access BRI Funds

BRI is generally implemented through BRI mutual funds or managers. For do-it-yourself investors who like to trade individual stocks, not many BRI research tools are available that are intended for direct use by the investing public. Currently, all BRI databases come with fairly expensive subscription fees, because a relatively small number of fund managers and advisors must absorb the cost of this research. I suspect this may change as demand continues to grow for the underlying BRI research, and as subscription costs follow the pattern of economies of scale to help bring down the fees per individual subscriber.

While investors with larger accounts (that is, over two million dollars) may enjoy some customization and the ability to select individual screening criteria á-la-carte through direct relationships with money managers, investors with smaller accounts must generally choose from among the available BRI funds that follow a predefined set of screens. The predefined BRI screens take a "big tent" approach by combining a careful selection of key issues that most evangelical Christians across denominations and traditions would agree are important.

The following chapter expands on the specific screening criteria used and what moral issues might trigger a red flag in the BRI databases.

4. DEFINING WHAT IS GOOD

> The ultimate measure of a person is not where they
> stand in moments of comfort and convenience, but
> where they stand at times of challenge and controversy.

> REV. DR. MARTIN LUTHER KING, JR.

Richard Stearns, the former Lenox CEO and current president
of World Vision, came to speak at my Rotary club in Spokane
shortly after his book *Hole in the Gospel*[14] was published. In his
address he said something that stuck with me: "How we invest
our money, talent, and energy is a moral decision." He was not
talking about BRI specifically, but his statement applies, and it
made an impact on me.

Even the smallest shareholder is an *owner* of the corporation
and is therefore accountable for the moral suitability of the company's products, services, and policies. As you pray through the
Scriptures, ask yourself if you know what your investment dollars are supporting. Can you do something to ensure that the
wealth entrusted to your management supports God-honoring
business activities? This is not meant to be an extra burden. BRI
creates an opportunity to shine light on corporate behavior and
to make our investing activities a part of our vital act of worship.
It is possible to do this all within the context of what is appropriate to your unique, personal needs and investing objectives.

If our chief aim in life is to glorify God in all we do, what if
we could also glorify God in how we considered our investment
choices?

Do My Hundred Shares Matter?

As we dive into a discussion around each of the BRI screens,
keep in mind that the central issue is *not* whether Christians

agree on the screens. The central issue is that, when it comes to investment decisions, too many Christian believers who love the Lord and seek to honor Him in every aspect of their lives are simply not thinking about screening at all.

This chapter really cuts to the root of the question, Why does BRI matter? It matters because we are called to live with integrity in all we do, including how we invest money entrusted to us as faithful stewards. It matters because we are called to be a light to a dark world. It matters because if every committed Christian thought this way about his or her investments, the collective impact of all Christians acting together might just change the global capital markets, and in turn change the world. (We will discuss this idea more in Chapter 8, "Collective Impact.")

> The call to action in this book is to search the Scriptures in prayer, talk with your financial advisor and pastor about BRI, and be faithful to what God is teaching you in this area.

THE EVOLUTION OF THE BRI SCREENS

If we think about BRI as a background-check system to screen investments, it raises the question, Who decides the screening categories, and why? It's important to understand that the predefined BRI screens evolved over time as various fund managers and watchdog organizations with screening databases began cooperating with each other to develop an industry around BRI. There is no "official" BRI organization or board of directors that decides these matters. Rather, an unofficial consensus crystallized slowly as database administrators and fund managers began to map out common ground with respect to key issues. More recently, a new nonprofit organization, the Christian Investment Forum, emerged to serve as a kind of trade association helping managers, advisors, and investors in the BRI community come together, share ideas, and create dialogue. We'll discuss the Christian Investment Forum in more detail in Chapter 7, "Demand Supply."

As addressed earlier in the book, the Christian faith is no stranger to differences in theology, thought, and traditions. However, there simply had to be some level of consensus and shared understanding in order for the screening databases, investment managers, and financial advisors to build solutions and help the BRI industry move forward. Imagine trying to build a house without a tape measure or some other standard of measurement. It would be impossible! Similarly, BRI pragmatically required some standard starting point, a model formed of wet clay that could be and still can be reshaped.

BRI SCREENS AT A GLANCE

The BRI Institute, founded by Rusty Leonard of Stewardship Partners, perhaps frames the predefined BRI screens most eloquently as an expression of God's love and compassion. According to the BRI Institute, BRI seeks to reflect:

- Justice and mercy for the defenseless
  - Abortion
  - Life-destroying or life-distorting scientific research
  - Persecuted Christians and oppressed peoples
- Justice and mercy for the poor
  - Any abuses of the poor, children, or the elderly
  - Political oppression
- Compassion for those addicted to and/or engaged in sinful lifestyles
  - Alcohol, gambling, tobacco
  - Pornography
  - Homosexuality

- Protection of marriage and the family
  - Entertainment seeking to destroy biblically based attitudes

In addition to negative screens (that is, avoiding companies that conflict with biblical principles), BRI also seeks to find companies that meet certain positive criteria (in addition to being an attractive investment financially). Examples include companies that show support for traditional Judeo-Christian values, quality products at fair prices, constructive stakeholder relations, a sustainable and healthy environment, and charitable giving to organizations not contrary to biblical teachings.

It is important to note that while the various providers of BRI have generally agreed on a predefined set of screens, each investment company or mutual fund that offers BRI may build on this shared framework by adding supplementary screens in other areas, or by implementing slight variations in screening priorities that may resonate uniquely with an investor's value system. For example, the Mennonites are a Protestant Christian faith group that began in the sixteenth century and are well known for their conviction concerning peacemaking and pacifism. Over one million members of the Mennonite church live out their faith in thorough detail, and we must respect those BRI funds developed in the Mennonite tradition which add additional screens to avoid investment in weaponry.

Others in the Christian community may only be concerned about avoiding defense companies that supply arms to enemies of Israel and the United States. In fact, the majority of BRI funds reflect such a view. As a matter of national security, you would hope this screen would be unnecessary for American defense contractors; however, the screen becomes more important when considering international stocks.

BRI Screening Model

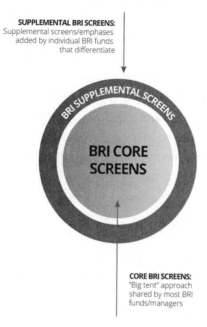

SUPPLEMENTAL BRI SCREENS:
Supplemental screens/emphases added by individual BRI funds that differentiate

BRI SUPPLEMENTAL SCREENS

BRI CORE SCREENS

CORE BRI SCREENS:
"Big tent" approach shared by most BRI funds/managers

Some BRI mutual funds add additional screening layers to monitor proxy votes for corporate accountability and executive compensation, based on the conviction that these are measures of good corporate stewardship. Without a doubt, each of the investment companies providing BRI has gone through a process of changes and adaptations to arrive at their current offerings.

---

*Any reference to the Eventide mutual funds is for illustrative purposes only in connection to historical, factual events and does not constitute an offer to buy or sell any security. Investing in any mutual fund involves risk, including possible loss of principal. For social, moral, and faith-based funds, returns may be lower than if the investor made decisions based solely on other investment considerations, but they could also be higher. Investors should consider the investment objectives, risks, charges, and expenses of the investment company carefully before investing. The prospectus and, if available, the summary prospectus contain this and other important information about the investment company.

Robin John, managing partner for Eventide Funds*, shared how Eventide Funds originated with eight core BRI screens and later began identifying other areas they felt were important in keeping with the spirit of BRI, avoiding, for example, human trafficking, high-end vanity products, or companies that outsource to other companies that employ child labor.

Eventide also began to focus on celebrating participation in companies that consciously create blessing and provision for all their stakeholders, in keeping with God's design. These stakeholders include customers, employees, host communities, supply chain, society, and environment. Robin John reflected, "For us at Eventide, it has been a process and we are still learning. Over time, what we have been convicted about is the basic teaching of Jesus Christ, which is to love God, and love our neighbor."

As a new believer, I once heard a sermon by Greg Laurie on John 15. In that chapter, Jesus calls the disciples together and shares that they are no longer servants but friends. Laurie goes on to describe how Christians sometimes approach friendship from a self-righteous perspective that goes something like this: "I don't smoke, and I don't chew, and I don't run with those who do." Laurie points out correctly that this is not the Jesus of the Bible. Jesus said in John 15:12, "My command is this: Love each other as I have loved you." Jesus was a friend to prostitutes and tax collectors, and had compassion on the poor. That is what the Christian life is all about—a life full of grace.

There is a key difference between, on the one hand, showing love and compassion for the addicted and downtrodden in society, and on the other hand, owning an establishment that profits from the addicted and downtrodden. Jesus had compassion on the prostitute, yet overturned tables and drove out the merchants in the temple. We are told to be a friend to those who are hurting, but not to profit from or take advantage of those who are hurting. BRI does not look down on corporations or their management from a prideful, self-righteous pedestal. Rather, BRI applies the negative screens with the intention of showing compassion toward the end users of the products and services that publicly traded corporations bring to the marketplace. BRI is a positive, practical application of God's call to love our neighbor.

A Closer Look

Now let's discuss each of the predefined BRI screens that have come to be included under the "big tent" approach—that is, the "core screens" among BRI funds. Keep in mind, the purpose of this chapter is not to convince you that each of these screens is good or bad. As a follower of Christ, you are probably already passionate about many of these issues. Some of these statistics may stimulate your conscience—and that is the point. My purpose for discussing each of the screens in detail is simply to help you make the connection between the issues we are already passionate about as committed Christians, and the realization that there may be companies in your investment portfolio that actively contradict your personal values, or that actively uphold your values. So here we go.

Abortion—There have been over fifty million abortions in the United States since abortion was first legalized in 1973.[15] That represents over 15 percent of America's current population.[16] According to the Guttmacher Institute, 1.21 million abortions were performed in the United States in 2008, the most recent year for which data is available.[17] This amounts to over three thousand abortions per day, each representing the end of a unique and precious life created by God.

> You formed my inward parts; you knitted me together in my mother's womb. I praise you, for I am fearfully and wonderfully made.
>
> PSALM 139:13–14, ESV

I remember being deeply affected in college by an educational video titled *The Silent Scream,* a 1984 documentary directed by Jack Duane Dabner.[18] The film captured in utero the abortion of a twelve-week-old fetus. Keep in mind that by the end of twelve weeks an unborn baby is fully formed in the womb; all the organs are formed, all limbs—including hands—are operational, and the baby can even suck his or her thumb at that time. The film showed ultrasound video of the baby kicking and moving around, hopelessly trying to escape the foreign probe. Then, in a moment of horror, the baby appeared to make an outcry of pain as it was terminated.

The video literally made me weep. An article in *Time* magazine reported that the film stirred so much emotion when it was first released that it made its way to the White House and was shown to then-president Ronald Reagan. President Reagan was quoted as saying, "If every member of Congress could see that film, they would move quickly to end the tragedy of abortion."[19]

The abortion BRI screen flags companies engaged in the manufacture, marketing, or licensing of abortifacients (substances used to voluntarily terminate pregnancy, such as mifepristone or RU–486); companies that perform abortion services; and companies boycotted for support of Planned Parenthood. In 2011, I had the opportunity to hear Abby Johnson share her dramatic, true story at an outreach event hosted by Life Services, a local life-affirming pregnancy resource center in Spokane. The event was so moving, I felt compelled to read Johnson's book, *Unplanned.*[20] My heart broke as she shared about her experiences as a former employee at Planned Parenthood, and how behind-closed-doors management told her to encourage abortions because it was a profit center for the organization. Her personal testimony and eye-opening faith journey is inspirational and courageous.

> "Blessed are those who mourn, for they shall be comforted."
>
> MATTHEW 5:4

The website for Planned Parenthood boasts, "For nearly 100 years, Planned Parenthood has promoted a common-sense approach to women's health and well-being."[21] What the website doesn't tell you is that over ninety years ago, Planned Parenthood was founded by Margaret Sanger, a racist and prolific writer closely tied to the eugenics movement in the 1920s. Eugenics was broadly defined as a commitment to breed out the "unfit" in society, specifically targeting racial minorities, the mentally and physically handicapped, and the criminally inclined. This evil philosophy was demonstrated most brutally in history by Hitler's Nazi army during World War II, and eugenics has since been discredited.

While Planned Parenthood has tried to distance itself from its eugenics past, the connection is still a topic of much controversy in the pro-life movement. The following is how Planned Parenthood describes itself today:

> We are a trusted health care provider, an informed educator, a passionate advocate, and a global partner… delivering vital reproductive health care, sex education, and information to millions of women, men, and young people worldwide.[22]

That sounds like a noble mission. However, the website fails to mention that Planned Parenthood is the largest abortion provider in the country. A couple of years ago, Planned Parenthood did a major marketing campaign in Spokane—with billboards and ads across various media—to portray Planned Parenthood as a broader health organization helping women with preventative care. Ironically, one such billboard that I frequently drove by had the picture of a woman from the waist up and the tagline, "Someone you know found a lump." The ad was likely alluding to breast cancer, but I could not help but wonder if the imagery and tagline may have been a Freudian slip. A "lump" is all that a fetus is, in the reasoning of the abortion business.

Abortion is big business. Planned Parenthood has an annual budget of one billion dollars and the director receives a salary of over one million dollars per year. Planned Parenthood is also a political machine, receiving over three hundred million dollars in funding from the federal government each year. State legislators, however, are beginning to get involved in the debate. In January 2013, *World* magazine published an article, "Roe v. Wade Turns 40," which highlighted how nineteen states enacted forty-three restrictions on abortion services in 2012, and ten states since 2011 have passed legislation or taken administrative action to strip abortion providers of tens of millions of dollars in taxpayer funding.[23]

As shareholders and therefore part-owners of a company, you are profiting from whatever it is that the company does. It's a simple fact. If a company makes a corporate donation to Planned Parenthood, then indirectly the shareholders of that company are assisting in the destruction of innocent lives. As Christ followers, we can do certain things to stand up for the defenseless unborn. We can carefully select political candidates every two and four years (First Story of stewardship), and support life-affirming organizations through personal giving (Second Story of stewardship).

Yet is it possible to indirectly and unknowingly support abortion with your investment dollars? The answer is yes. The shocking truth is that a person may be peacefully protesting in front of a Planned Parenthood clinic, out of their love and compassion for the unborn, and at the same time unwittingly funding Planned Parenthood via corporate donations inside their mutual fund holdings. BRI attempts to shine a light into this area so that investors are informed and empowered to avoid companies that continue to fund Planned Parenthood. If you could help it, would you want even one dollar of your portfolio invested in a company that promotes or profits from abortion?

> For a current list of companies contributing to Planned Parenthood, visit www.fightpp.org.

Human Rights and Trafficking—Human rights violations are also closely monitored by the predefined BRI screens. For example, a company using child slave labor in the developing world to manufacture blue jeans would be screened out of a BRI portfolio. It is astounding to consider that, according to the International Justice Mission, there are more than twenty-seven million slaves in the world today. In fact, more children, women, and men are held in slavery right now than over the course of the entire transatlantic slave trade, and trafficking in humans generates profits in excess of thirty-two billion dollars per year for those who, by force or deception, sell human beings into slavery and sexual bondage.[24]

Learn to do good. Seek justice. Help the oppressed. Defend the cause of orphans. Fight for the rights of widows.

Isaiah 1:17, NLT

The Bible is clear that we as Christian believers are to steer clear of companies that violate basic human rights. As our own country's Declaration of Independence so eloquently affirms, all men, women, and children are created equal and are endowed by God with certain inalienable rights, including the right to life and liberty.[25]

Environment—The environment is also an important factor in the BRI screens. Remember back to our foundational principle from Psalm 24:1: "The earth is the LORD's and everything in it"—and we are managers of His resources. One emphasis of BRI is on sustainability, which is defined by *Merriam-Webster's Dictionary* as "a method of harvesting or using a resource so that the resource is not depleted or permanently damaged." For example, the BRI screens allow for investment in energy, timber, and mining companies that take environmental sustainability seriously. So the BRI perspective on the environment differs from the more liberal fringes of the conservation movement, which generally have zero tolerance for any environmental disruption, whether sustainable or not.

Alcohol—You may be surprised to see alcohol as a screen. After all, wine has been God's gift to man for thousands of years. It is a gift, but as with all things good, God has laid down some ground rules calling for personal responsibility. Jesus drank the fruit of the vine (Matthew 26:20), and Paul suggested that Timothy drink a little wine for health problems (1 Timothy 5:23).

Even though for some of us it may be acceptable to drink alcohol in moderation, there's a good case for its inclusion as part of the screening process.

Alcoholism statistics in the United States remain more than a little concerning. An article from the *American Journal of Public Health* notes that easy access—in this case the term means cheap prices—is a contributing factor in the development of alcohol-related emotional, social, and health problems and deaths. In the United States, 15.3 million Americans meet the criteria for an alcohol use disorder, according to the NESARC*.[26] And information from the World Health Organization shows there are an estimated 140 million alcoholics around the world! Additionally, alcohol use remains prevalent among today's teenagers. According to SADD†, during the last thirty days, 26.4 percent of underage persons (ages twelve to twenty) used alcohol, and the incidence of binge drinking among the same group was 17.4 percent.[27]

I have witnessed the dangers of both underage drinking and addiction. In college, I joined a social fraternity before I became a believer in Christ. And after trusting Jesus, I ended up staying in the house in order to minister to those in the Greek system through a Cru ministry called Greek Life. One weekend in particular, a neighboring house around the corner on fraternity row held an overnight retreat that combined cliff diving and alcohol. You can guess where this story is going. The campus newspaper reported that everyone had been drinking heavily, and one of the freshman pledges did not surface from the cliff dive. So an older member of the fraternity dove in after

---

*National Epidemiologic Survey on Alcohol and Related Conditions (NESARC)
†Students Against Destructive Decisions (SADD)

him in a rescue attempt. Both drowned. Alcohol manufacturers often glamorize excessive drinking in TV advertising to boost sales, but in truth there is nothing glamorous about drinking irresponsibly.

Another personal experience that resonates strongly with the predefined BRI screen on alcohol is a lesson I learned from my grandfather, Thomas Bruce Graham (1929–2009). He served as lieutenant colonel of the United States Marine Corps and saw action on the shores of Okinawa, Japan during World War II. After the war, he earned his college degree from USC and by the 1960s had become a partner at Dean Witter in Los Angeles (a company now merged into Morgan Stanley). Over time, my grandfather built a very respectable practice at Dean Witter and for many years enjoyed life as a successful stock broker in Pasadena, California.

But this was also the era of martini lunches, now romanticized on the retro TV series *Mad Men*. To make a long story short, drinking got the best of my grandfather and he lost everything. His career, the house, his marriage to my grandmother. Everything. By the grace of God, through Alcoholics Anonymous he broke his addiction, rekindled his faith in the Lord, and married my step-grandmother, remaining dry for the thirty years they were married to each other.

I have friends who won't go near alcohol because they too have been touched by alcoholism in some way, either through a family member or someone they know. Alcohol is a drug, and as with any addiction, alcoholism can have destructive and long-lasting effects. So it is with a spirit of humility that I approach such a sensitive subject as alcohol. The decision whether to drink, perhaps in moderation, is a personal choice we each need to make for ourselves.

So whether you eat or drink or whatever you do, do it all for the glory of God.

1 Corinthians 10:31

Are alcohol companies evil? No, of course not. Those who follow this BRI screen simply decline to participate as investor-owners. While most of us can moderate our personal consumption as individuals—and federal and state laws attempt to limit distribution— avoiding profits from sales to addicts and underage drinkers is a reasonable choice because manufacturers, and by extension shareholders, cannot control alcohol's abuse. Most wineries and microbreweries are operated privately, either as a family business or by a vintner committed to producing quality over quantity. Publicly traded alcohol companies, on the other hand, are for the most part in the high-volume business. College kids and adults with addictions typically gravitate toward low-cost alcohol they can buy in bulk, such as what you see advertised at local minimarts—boxes stacked in pyramids, selling for less than a dollar per can. Regardless of how you choose to moderate alcohol in your own life, the question is simple: if you could choose, would you want to participate in corporate profits derived partially from alcohol sales to underage drinkers and adults with addictions?

Tobacco—French mathematician Blaise Pascal (1623–1662) made the argument that we were created to have a dependency on God. He wrote:

"What else does this craving, and this helplessness, proclaim but that there was once in man a true happiness, of which all that now remains is the empty print and trace? This he tries in vain to fill with everything around him…though none can help, since this infinite abyss can be filled only with an infinite and immutable object; in other words by God himself."[28]

We can fill the vacuum with other things, but nothing else will ultimately satisfy that longing of the soul except God. It has been proven that tobacco, like all physically addictive drugs, changes the chemical makeup of the brain and creates a biological dependency. Once popularized in the 1940s through clever advertising and Hollywood glamour as a symbol of status, smoking has now become a symbol for death and disease. Thanks to the Ad Council and classroom education, younger generations of smokers can no longer plead ignorance. Yet people keep smoking. The appeal is a mystery to me.

> Do you not know that your body is a temple of the Holy Spirit, who is in you, whom you have received from God? You are not your own; you were bought at a price. Therefore honor God with your body.

> 1 CORINTHIANS 6:19–20

According to a report by the World Lung Foundation in 2012, tobacco-related deaths have nearly tripled in the past decade and "big tobacco firms are undermining public efforts that could save millions."[29] Tobacco has killed fifty million people in the last ten years, and according to the WLF and the American Cancer Society, if current trends continue, a billion people will die from tobacco use and exposure this century—one person every six seconds. Michael Eriksen, one of the authors of that report, said that although smoking rates are declining in developed countries, smoking in poorer regions of the world—where, by the way, tobacco is less regulated—is off the charts.

Some Christians do not see a problem with the persistence of tobacco sales despite all we know today about the dangers of smoking. You could make a case to avoid smoking based on 1 Corinthians 6:20, which calls us to "honor God" with how we treat our bodies. But that same argument could also apply to all sorts of harmful self-indulgences, ranging from the food we eat to, in my case, not getting enough exercise. That is where I believe personal responsibility comes into play.

We are all accountable to God for the choices we make, including those that result in harm to ourselves. The main reason tobacco is included in the BRI screen, however, is because tobacco companies profit from a product that causes harm to others, especially the poor. I have a Christian colleague and friend who agrees with me that smoking is bad and essentially a tax on the poor, yet still feels it is okay to own stock in a major tobacco company. Yet before I rush to cast judgment, I have only to remember that there was a time in my career, not too long ago, when I would not have thought twice about owning tobacco stock either. Since learning about BRI, I have become a lot more intentional about what industries I am supporting, either directly or indirectly, through my investments.

Regardless of where you stand on the smoking debate, why choose to profit from an addictive product responsible for the deaths of millions around the world, when there are so many other investment opportunities that do not cause harm to our neighbor?

Gambling—Mark Twain shrewdly observed that "the best throw at dice is to throw them away."[30] Gambling addiction is a chronic condition, similar to alcoholism or drug addiction, according to Medline Plus.[31] The National Council on Problem Gambling estimates that two million Americans, or about 1 percent of the population, are pathological gamblers. An additional 2 to 3 percent, or four to six million people, would be considered problem gamblers—people whose gambling affects their everyday lives.[32]

Gambling is big business. Americans spend more on gambling than on major league baseball, somewhere in the vicinity of 550 billion dollars per year.[33] In one way or another, gaming companies play a role in feeding or enabling gambling addiction, which affects millions of people. And a large percentage of the repeat patrons at casinos are lower-income people thinking incorrectly that if they keep coming back, they have a better chance of hitting the jackpot.

For the American who travels to Las Vegas once every few years for the food, and who recreationally spends maybe twenty dollars on the nickel slots for entertainment, it may be hard to comprehend the mental prison in which a gambling addict lives. Yet in my college days, I saw first-hand just how destructive gambling could be. When I was a freshman, a senior in the fraternity had a gambling problem, and at one of the chapter meetings he shared a story about one of his darkest moments. He had gotten in over his head at the race track and received a very real threat on his life if he didn't pay back his gambling debts. With nowhere else to turn, the fraternity voted to suspend food catering service and scrounged together enough money to help him. The condition, of course, was that he seek out help for his gambling addiction. Sadly, even after that traumatic experience and further counseling, he continued to struggle with gambling for years.

The predefined BRI screen for gambling essentially challenges us with the question: could we invest in other areas that do not profit from human weakness and gambling addiction?

Pornography—Pornography has reached epidemic levels in this country, and its casualties include wrecked marriages, sexually abused children, and adults with pornography addictions. In 2006 porn was a ninety-seven-billion-dollar industry worldwide and a thirteen-billion-dollar industry in the US, at one time exceeding the combined revenues of ABC, CBS, and NBC.[34] Those numbers have decreased substantially in recent years as a result of free online pornography and rampant piracy.

Nevertheless, in a 2012 survey porn revenues in the US still exceeded five billion dollars.[35] Those figures represent revenue from all forms of content delivery, such as sales and rental of DVDs, membership-based websites, video-on-demand, live webcams, satellite and cable pay-per-views, and so on. Porn still earns big bucks, and it is having a dramatic impact on culture. According to recent statistics, 90 percent of children ages eight to sixteen have viewed porn, 70 percent of all American men ages eighteen to thirty-four visit a porn site each month, and one in six women struggle with porn addiction. Over 25 percent of search-engine requests are for porn, and 38 percent of adults now say that porn is morally acceptable.[36] According to the Family Research Council, 56 percent of divorces involve one spouse's continued use of Internet pornography.[37]

The statistics are overwhelming. Porn is a cancer in our society that has spread fast and out of control. While the Internet is a powerful tool for commerce and creative collaboration, porn is one of its darker sides. Similar to the way Henry Ford brought the automobile within reach of millions of Americans with the invention of the assembly line and mass production techniques, the Internet boom has expanded pornography "production" exponentially by making it readily accessible to every household in the world with just a few clicks of a mouse. As a Christian believer, is it okay to profit from human weakness and pornography addiction?

Lifestyle and Sexuality—BRI attempts to limit investment in companies that use shareholder dollars to promote sex outside of marriage, or that celebrate and support "alternative lifestyles" that the Bible describes as immoral.

When I was in college, I read Neil Clark Warren's book *Finding the Love of your Life*, based on Christian perspectives on dating and courtship. Warren's book changed my entire philosophy on the purpose of dating. Warren rejects the modern notion of casual dating and advocates instead becoming intentional about what qualities to seek in a lifelong mate. Another book that guided my view of marriage based on biblical principles was *Life on the Edge* by Dr. James Dobson.[38] I highly recommend both works for the First Story of our House analogy.

I am thankful to have met my wife by pursuing marriage this way, despite my many weaknesses and shortcomings. God is gracious. Years after his book's publication, Warren took its concepts and translated them into an online dating service, *eHarmony.com*. Many of my Christian friends have found their soul mates through eHarmony.com and similar quality sites, and now enjoy thriving marriages.

Unfortunately, sin will take what is good and pervert it. In C.S. Lewis's fictional work *The Screwtape Letters,* which is written from the perspective of two demons seeking to sabotage God's work, the mentor demon writes this to his disciple:

> [God] has filled His world full of pleasures. There are things for humans to do all day long without His minding in the least—sleeping, washing, eating, drinking,

making love, playing, praying, working....Everything has to be twisted before it's any use to us [demons].

In February 2011, *Bloomberg Magazine* (formerly known as *BusinessWeek*) ran a cover story about AshleyMadison, another kind of online dating company.[39] The only rule for getting an online dating profile at AshleyMadison is that you have to already be married. The homepage of the website reads, "Life is short. Have an affair." Shocking, right? I don't know what is more disheartening, the fact that a service like this even exists in the first place, or that it has attracted twenty-two million subscribers.[40]

There's no question that our culture is under attack, and corporations follow where the demand leads. It's difficult to get an accurate read on adultery statistics due to the discreet nature of the sin itself, but US Census data documents over two million marriages per year,[41] and according to Focus on the Family, the number of marriages that end in divorce ranges from 40 to 50 percent.[42] With such a high percentage of divorce caused by infidelity (second only to divorce related to money issues), just think of the potential market! If a company like that ever had an Initial Public Offering (IPO), would you buy shares? No matter how great the investment opportunity, AshleyMadison certainly fails the BRI screen. As Christ followers, we would avoid such an investment out of love and compassion for the victims of adultery, and because it is in clear conflict with biblical principles. It would simply be wrong to profit from sin and the destruction of families.

Much debate is currently stirring this country over the definition of marriage and the role of lifestyle and sexuality in society. In the state of Washington, where I live, same-sex marriage was legalized in the 2012 election by a majority vote of the people, 53.7 percent to 46.3 percent.[43] The Christian faith teaches that marriage is a sacred institution purposed and ordained by God. In contrast, our modern culture has reduced marriage to a ritual couples go through after they have been living together for a while. In the movie *The Invention of Lying,* a young couple prepares the following wedding vows:

> We are here today…to share in the wedding of Brad and Anna, two attractive young people who have come to the conclusion that this wedding will be mutually beneficial.…Brad, do you agree to stay with Anna for as long as you want to, and to protect your offspring for as long as you can? (I do.) And, Anna, do you agree to stay with Brad for as long as you want to, and to protect your offspring for as long as you can? (I do.)[44]

The movie was intended as a satire on religion, but it contains a profound truth: apart from God and His purpose for the institution, marriage is not all that meaningful. If this is any reflection of our culture, it is not that big a leap to understand why voters in Washington and other states have laws that further secularize the definition of marriage. For the Christ follower, however, the exchange of marriage vows is more than just a legal formality. It is a covenant before God we should honor and sustain in keeping with the teachings of His Word.

It's important to remember that even in the state of Washington, where same-sex marriage was voted into law, over 1.4 million Washington citizens voted no. What BRI is advocating is that publicly-traded corporations, at a minimum, remain neutral on controversial public policy issues, such as the radical GLBT (Gay Lesbian Bisexual Transsexual) agenda. The agenda is radical because it seeks to erase gender completely.

For example, the introduction of unisex bathroom laws in

certain cities[45]—that's radical, extreme. It is not about freedoms or human rights. Otherwise, GLBT advocacy groups would be satisfied with domestic partner benefits laws that have emerged in recent years. As committed Christians, we believe that God's design is for marriage to be between one man and one woman, and that both are created in God's image. This comes directly from Genesis, the first book in the Bible. The radical GLBT agenda is to redefine the institution of marriage and create a gender-neutral society, which is in direct contradiction to the Christian faith tradition and biblical principles. The question is whether supporting that agenda, directly or indirectly, is okay for the committed Christian. That is the essence of the BRI screen for lifestyle and sexuality. BRI databases do not penalize companies for complying with federal or state marriage and domestic partner laws, but they do screen out companies that make donations to or sponsor events for advocacy groups that promote the radical GLBT agenda.

This BRI screen relating to alternative family lifestyles hits close to home for me because I have a half-brother who lives an openly gay lifestyle. Over the years we have had many interesting discussions about faith and life. My brother knows that I love him unconditionally, both as a brother and as a precious child of God. In the book *God Space*,[46] Doug Pollock makes an important distinction—acceptance does not mean endorsement. Pollock's book is not specifically about sexuality, but more generally about coming alongside people wherever they are in life and creating safe environments for them to discover the love of God. Accepting my brother and disagreeing with his behaviors are not mutually exclusive. I know that God loves my brother, just as I recognize the Bible's unmistakable clarity on the subject of sexuality.

For that matter, the Bible is clear on many other moral issues our culture has chosen to ignore. The reality is that all sin separates us from God. I have heard the analogy that God's Law is like a pane of glass, and any sin is like a hammer blow to the glass. No matter where you strike the glass, the entire pane shatters. We've all violated God's standards of right and wrong, and we deserve to be separated from God forever. The good news is that Christ, by his sacrificial death, paid that penalty for us and bridged the gap between us and God. In response to the love and forgiveness freely offered to us, we are called to turn from sin and choose a life that honors Him. Obedience is our spiritual act of worship.

I don't pretend to understand the daily struggle of a Christ-follower who battles with the temptation of attraction to the same sex. That is a subject for an entirely different book. But I do take the Bible seriously when it says that the gay lifestyle is contrary to His will and design.

BRI is not about persecuting the gay community. Christ calls us to love. In John 8, Jesus encountered a woman who had been caught in the act of adultery. Under Old Testament law, the woman was sentenced to be stoned to death. Jesus stood in front of the woman, an angry crowd of religious leaders ready to stone her, and said, "Let he who is without sin cast the first stone" (John 8:7). One by one the men dropped their stones and walked away. "Jesus stood up and said to her, 'Where are they? Has no one condemned you?' She said, 'No one, Lord.' And Jesus said, 'Neither do I condemn you; go, and from now on sin no more'" (8:10–11). This story is a lesson in both forgiveness and the inviolability of the Bible's moral standards. Notice that Jesus never condoned the woman's sin, nor those of anyone else; in fact, He clearly instructed her to "sin no more." Yet it is also a lesson in accepting that God alone is judge.

I had always seen this story from the perspective of the

woman about to be stoned, but a pastor once illuminated the other side of the story—the story of the men who, one by one, dropped their stones and walked away. I think we have all been on both sides of that equation at various times—either in desperate need of forgiveness, or poised to cast stones at others. BRI is not about throwing stones; it's about ensuring that we, through our investment dollars, aren't participating in the attack upon and undermining of biblical truth and morality. As Christ followers, we are called to take a stand for truth. In this country, our freedoms and laws are ultimately decided by the will of the people, as guided by our constitution. While the debate over marriage continues to work its way through the political process, the question is whether you would be okay with your investment dollars funding advocacy groups in their efforts to advance the radical GLBT agenda.

In fall of 2012, JC Penney* made headline news. Sales were down 20 percent, and NBC reported that the blame for this sharp decline in sales was due to the new CEO's strategy to eliminate coupon clipping deals.[47] What the news failed to correlate was that during the same time period, JC Penney launched a series of controversial advertising campaigns that prompted One Million Moms, an organization closely associated with the conservative American Family Association, to boycott JC Penney products. The ad that sparked all this controversy featured a same-sex couple laughing and playing with their children. The text of the ad read: "What makes Dad so cool? He's the swim coach, tent maker, best friend, bike fixer and hug giver—all rolled into one. Or two." In a prepared statement, One Million Moms responded, "It's obvious that JC Penney would rather take

---

*Any reference to JC Penney is for illustrative purposes only in connection to historical, factual events and does not constitute a recommendation to buy or sell any security. See also important disclosures.

sides than remain neutral in the culture war. JC Penney will pay for this at the cash register."[48]

Companies are mindful of the power of a boycott. What most people don't realize is that if just 3 percent of a company's customers boycott a product, it could translate into 10–20 percent of profits. That's just how the math works out, because much of a company's expenses are fixed and the bills must be paid before a company can calculate its profit. Was the bargain-shopping world really offended by the end of coupons, or more so by JC Penney's challenge to traditional family values?

Home Depot* is another example of a publicly traded company that has chosen to use shareholder resources to support the radical GLBT agenda. According to the American Family Association, Home Depot has given financial and corporate support for open displays of GLBT activism on main streets in American towns. Rather than remain neutral, Home Depot has chosen to sponsor and participate in numerous gay pride parades and festivals, including "Kids Workshops."[49] In May 2012, the AFA delivered over a quarter-million petition signatures to Home Depot chairman Frank Blake during the company's annual shareholder meeting, in connection with an organized boycott which lasted nearly three years. While Home Depot has since reduced its donations to GLBT groups, Home Depot's official response to the boycott was that they have not made any changes to their policies and have no intention of directing their associates to discontinue participation in Pride or other GLBT community events.[50]

As corporations become more and more politically active and socially engaged over issues that run contrary to biblical

---

* Any reference to Home Depot is for illustrative purposes only in connection to historical, factual events and does not constitute a recommendation to buy or sell any security. See also important disclosures.

principles, values-based investing, and particularly BRI, may have an important role to play in influencing corporate behavior and the future of the capital markets. We'll discuss this more in Chapter 8, "Collective Impact." In the meantime, BRI presents a values-alignment opportunity to the individual investor: if you had a choice, would you want to profit from companies that are using your investment dollars to advance political agendas contrary to your faith values?

Video games—Grand Theft Auto is one of the top ten video games in all-time sales, having sold over fifty million copies. Frequently cited in the press is game action in which players carjack a vehicle, pick up a prostitute, have (implied) sex with the prostitute, and then kill her and steal her money. What is less commonly known is that the maker of the game is a publicly traded company on the NASDAQ exchange. Is it possible this company could be in your portfolio?

In the wake of the 2012 Sandy Hook Elementary tragedy in Newtown, Connecticut, CNBC's *Street Signs* ran a report about the possible link between violent video games and tragic shooting crimes. While you can't blame these horrific events on violent TV and video games alone, it does make you wonder. The US is the world's biggest video game market, with over one hundred million players and more than five million kids who spend over forty hours a week playing video games. In 2011 alone, Americans spent just shy of twenty-five billion dollars on video games, gaming hardware, and accessories.[51]

What's the big deal? CNBC reported that studies now link violent video games to higher levels of aggression. The three top-selling video games are all violent, where "the player is a shooter and his challenge is to kill."[52] The most popular video game franchise of all time, Call of Duty®, is also owned by a publicly traded company. It grossed over one billion dollars in just fifteen days after its November 2012 release of *Black Ops II*, with over 150 million hours logged online by people playing the game on Xbox® LIVE® and PlayStation Network.[53]

Are all video games bad? Do all gamers feel the need to carry out physical acts of violence? Of course not. These platforms provide amazing educational tools for kids, not to mention learning apps for the iPad and other devices. It all comes back to parents taking responsibility for determining what content is appropriate for their children. For example, you might decide that blasting away aliens and fantasy creatures is more reasonable than simulating carjacking vehicles and shooting at prostitutes.

How does this all relate to BRI? Simply ask the question, Would I want my investments to profit from a game I might not permit my children to play?

Shining Light in a Dark World

As I researched these facts and statistics around the predefined BRI screens, I couldn't help wondering why a loving God would allow suffering and sin in the world. This is a profound mystery to me, but one principle rings true. In the words of Dr. Bill Robinson, "God gives us the freedom to choose, and when that kind of freedom is placed in the hands of sinful humanity, there will be evil in the world."

There is no question these statistics can be depressing, but keep reading and you will see that the "depressing" truth can become part of the formula for personal and cultural victory for God. It's also possible that, while this wasn't my purpose for sharing this research, some of what you've learned is convicting. If that's the case for you, remember the most important truth—

we serve a God of amazing love and grace. First John 1:9 says, "If we confess our sins, he is faithful and just and will forgive us our sins and purify us from all unrighteousness." Every true Jesus follower has availed himself or herself of God's forgiveness and cleansing at least once, and the original grammar of John's statement implies that we need this spiritual bath regularly, because we all sin every day. This is a humbling reality.

And yet in our humility, God calls us still to shine His light in dark places. How can we, who were ourselves rescued from sin, presume to stand and speak for truth in the world? Isn't this self-righteousness? In his book *Incarnate Leadership,* Bill Robinson offers an analogy to describe how Christians, who must assume an attitude of humility, can at the same time affect positive change in the environments around them. He explains that the light of truth and righteousness originates not with us, but with God. We, who were ourselves delivered from darkness, are now mirrors that reflect His light. "Our job," he says, "is to keep the mirror angled between God and darkness,"[54] never boasting any righteousness from ourselves, but reflecting God's truth and righteousness into a world that desperately needs them.

Perhaps some of these topics are stirring a passionate response in you. The purpose of including these statistics is to emphasize that our investment choices really do matter. As we wrap up our overview of the predefined BRI screens, my hope is that this chapter helped you make the connection between issues you are already passionate about as a committed Christian, and the realization that your investment portfolio may include companies that actively violate your Bible-based convictions. Even if you only agreed with some of the predefined screens, BRI is still compatible as an opportunity for alignment of investments with values. A competent financial advisor who is knowledgeable about BRI will be able to help you evaluate the nuances in screening approaches among the various BRI providers and find a BRI solution that is the right fit for your needs and objectives.

Perhaps this entire chapter can be boiled down to this: if you wouldn't write a check for one dollar in support of these unbiblical causes, products, or services, why would you want your investment dollars funding them?

5. MYTH BUSTING

> Sow your seed in the morning, and at evening let not
> your hands be idle, for you do not know which will
> succeed, whether this or that, or whether both will do
> equally well.

ECCLESIASTES 11:6

In the process of investigating BRI, I had many conversations
with clients, colleagues, and mentors as sounding boards to help
formulate my opinion and get a pulse on the industry's understanding of the concept. Among the range of responses I
received, a trend began to emerge that didn't fit with the latest
research data—a collection of stubborn misperceptions. In fact,
I discovered that many of the stereotypes being propagated
about BRI were outdated or otherwise inaccurate. The following
is just a brief summary of some of the most common myths I
encountered in my research.

MYTH #1: PERFORMANCE WILL SUFFER

When I talk to investors and other financial advisors about investing from a values-based perspective, I always seem to encounter
the impression that investors will surely take a bath on performance. I recently spoke with a friend in the BRI community, Dwight
Short, as to why investors might so consistently expect a poor
financial outcome. Dwight is the author of *Kingdom Gains* and
Profit or Principles, having recently retired from a long career of
thirty-four years at Merrill Lynch*, where he and his partners
managed over six hundred million dollars in client assets. He said
to me, "I think it is driven partly by financial advisors who allow

---

*Any reference to Merrill Lynch is for illustrative purposes only in connection with his-
torical, factual events and does not constitute an offer to buy or sell any security.

their clients to think that way, and partially by the media, who often put out ill-informed information. So it's a variety of things, but it all centers back on, to me, greed, to one degree or another. Not excessive greed but it's still greed. You don't want to lose. You don't want to miss out."

Dwight went on to say, "I also think there's a fear among advisors that they are going to drive business away, and a fear that they are going to stand out by being different. And if that difference turns into underperformance, then I think that they are fearful of losing clients. I will tell you, I think that fear is very ill-founded. Because when you present BRI properly, people are very clear on whether or not they want to be 'all-in'. I had more Jewish clients who said, 'Hey, Dwight, if you really believe in this stuff, let's go all-in with it.' And I had some Christian clients who were very reluctant, saying, 'Uh, I don't know—that sounds too liberal for me or too conservative or whatever.' And I think that excuse is a smokescreen; they just didn't want to get an inferior return."

The truth is, investors can realistically expect to address their needs and objectives within the framework of BRI. Of course, past performance is not a guarantee of future results, and all investing involves risk. Yet several recent research studies have compared performance between screened and non-screened portfolios, and the results are compelling.

Martin Wildy, CFA and senior analyst for ARIS Corporation, described two key research studies in a recent white paper, "The Performance Costs of Social Screening."[55] In the first, a 2008 study, "The Wages of Social Responsibility," Meir Statman and Denys Glushkov focused on answering this question by analyzing the returns of stocks rated by social responsibility over a fifteen-year period (1992-2007). This study found that tilting a portfolio toward stocks that were rated highly on such socially responsible characteristics as community, environment, and employee relations provided an advantage over conventional investors. This advantage was largely offset by excluding stocks in sectors such as tobacco, alcohol, gambling, and weapons. The net effect was no material impact.

In the second, a 2011 study, "Socially Screened Portfolios: An Attribution Analysis of Relative Performance," Lloyd Kurtz and Dan BiBartolomeo statistically analyzed the performance of the KLD 400 Social Index* relative to the S&P 500 Index* from 1992 to 2010. The authors determined that any performance differences are fully explained by conventional investment factors. According to the authors, "General assumptions of reduced return are wrong and investors do not sacrifice long-term returns when pursuing corporate social responsibility." To be fair, the KLD 400 uses slightly different screening criteria than BRI, which we address in Chapter 6, "Back to Values: A Historical Perspective."

In another independent research study conducted by BRI Institute (BRII) in 2013, the historical performance of individual companies in the S&P 500 that passed the BRI screens were compared to the historical performance of individual companies

---

*The Standard & Poor's 500 Index is a capitalization weighted index of 500 stocks designed to measure performance of the broad domestic economy through changes in the aggregate market value of 500 stocks representing all major industries.

The MSCI KLD 400 Social Index comprises companies with high Environmental, Social and Governance (ESG) ratings and excludes companies involved in Alcohol, Gambling, Tobacco, Military Weapons, Civilian Firearms, Nuclear Power, Adult Entertainment, and Genetically Modified Organisms (GMO). The Index aims to serve as a benchmark for investors whose objectives include owning companies with very high ESG ratings and avoiding companies that are incompatible with specific values-based criteria. Launched in May 1990 as the Domini 400 Social Index, it is one of the first Socially Responsible Investing (SRI) indexes. Constituent selection is based on data from MSCI ESG Research.

Indexes are unmanaged and cannot be invested into directly. Unmanaged index returns do not reflect fees, expenses, or sales charges. Index performance is not indicative of the performance of any investment. Past performance is no guarantee of future results.

Saints Versus Sinners in the S&P 500
Cumulative Returns of Stocks Passing BRI Screens vs. Those Failing
1/1/2001 – 3/31/2013

that failed the BRI screens over a period from January 2001 to March 2013.[56] The conclusion of the study was that there was no statistically meaningful difference in performance between the basket of companies that passed the BRI screens and the basket of companies that failed the BRI screens.

It's important to note that, according to the BRI Institute, BRI screens eliminate somewhere between 20 and 40 percent of S&P 500* companies, depending on the time period. On the conservative end of that range, that still leaves over three hundred large US companies available for investment. According to the eVALUEator, a BRI database developed by the Timothy

Source: Bloomberg, Stewardship Partners. The screened results presented above are simulated and do not correspond to any real investment product. Simulated performace data is hypothetical and provided for information purposes only. It does not reflect actual performance and is gross of any fees. This document is not an offer to buy or sell securrities. Past performance is not indicative of future results. The number of companies screened out of the S&P 500 during the test period ranged from a low of 72 to a more recent high of 209 (out of 500).

*The Standard & Poor's 500 Index (S&P 500) is a capitalization weighted index of 500 stocks designed to measure performance of the broad domestic economy through changes in the aggregate market value of 500 stocks representing all major industries. All performance referenced is gross of any fees. Past performance is not indicative of future results.

Plan, only 6.5 percent of the ten thousand publicly traded companies (including both US and foreign companies) violate the BRI screens.[57] That means over 9,300 companies of all sizes around the world are available for investment within the BRI framework. Statistically speaking, a portfolio needs only around thirty individual stocks to adequately diversify for the risk of any one company blowing up (such as from an unexpected lawsuit or news-breaking scandal). Managers still have a vast universe of thousands of publicly traded companies from which to choose when building a well-diversified portfolio that passes the BRI screens.

Based on a review of academic research and on comparison of index returns, there is no historical evidence that investors should expect social screening to materially impact long-term performance, either positively or negatively. To be fair, returns could be lower with Biblically Responsible Investing than if the adviser made decisions based solely on other investment considerations, but they could also be higher.

George Schwartz, president of Schwartz Investment Counsel and the Ave Maria* family of funds, makes the argument that there is actually a strong relationship between ethics and business results. In his book *Good Returns,*[58] he writes, "Over time, those companies that are well managed—that deal ethically with suppliers, employees, and customers—are the ones that tend to be the most successful, and morality is a vital component of

---

*Any reference to the Ave Maria mutual funds is for illustrative purposes only in connection to historical, factual events and does not constitute an offer to buy or sell any security. Investing in any mutual fund involves risk, including possible loss of principal. For social, moral, and faith-based funds, returns may be lower than if the investor made decisions based solely on other investment considerations, but they could also be higher. Investors should consider the investment objectives, risks, charges, and expenses of the investment company carefully before investing. The prospectus and, if available, the summary prospectus contain this and other important information about the investment company.

good management." The book title, *Good Returns,* is of course a play on words that underscores a valid point: by pursuing companies that operate ethically, in alignment with BRI principles, Schwartz expects his performance to be better, not worse.

MYTH #2: PERFORMANCE DOESN'T MATTER

The truth is, performance does matter. Stewardship is a two-sided coin: it is about earning a return on investment, and also about how we earn it. Good stewardship upholds both, emphasizing one without sacrificing the other. I don't think the Lord would be happy with us if we squandered all His resources, and then tried to justify it by saying, "Yeah, but look at all the bad companies we avoided." Remember the parable of the talents in Matthew 25:15–30. In the story, a rich master, about to depart on a journey, gives each of three servants money (a certain number of *talents*, a measure of weight), which they are instructed to manage until his return. Two of the servants show a profit, garnering praise for their initiative. But when the third servant merely hands back the original amount with which he had been entrusted, the master is incensed. Why, he demands, did the servant bury the money in the ground when he might have at least deposited it with the bankers to earn interest? In the parable, the faithless servant answers: he was afraid.

Benjamin Graham (1894-1976), a British-born American economist, was the first proponent of value-investing—that is, value in monetary terms, not moral value. In his groundbreaking book *Securities Analysis* (1934), Graham wisely expressed that markets are primarily driven by a mixture of reason and emotion—namely fear and greed.[59] It is human nature to fear, but fear rarely leads to good planning. Neither does greed, for that matter. More often than not, either emotion will lead us into trouble. Jesus' parable agrees, with respect to fear.

But what about greed? The parable explicitly attests that rightly motivated stewardship invests with the intention of making resources grow. Is this different from greed? Yes. Greed is akin to selfish ambition—gain for one's own sake—whereas a servant or steward labors for the sake of his master. Outwardly you might see both individuals working with the same energy and activity; but if you recognize who benefits most directly from the hard work, you understand the important distinction. One does it for himself while the other does it for someone else. In business, consider how an employee might be promoted to the position of manager—by putting the good of the company ahead of him or herself.

> His master replied, "Well done, good and faithful servant! You have been faithful with a few things; I will put you in charge of many things. Come and share your master's happiness!"

> MATTHEW 25:23

Note that in the parable, the illustrated examples are extremes. On the one hand, the servant with the five talents doubled his money, while the one who buried his one talent earned zero. Expressed as an internal rate of return, the range is from zero percent to 100 percent. Imagine if the parable had gone like this: One servant went out and earned an 8-percent return dishonestly and caused harm to his neighbor, while another servant came back with a 6-percent return that was earned justly and honorably. Who might the Lord reward in that scenario? Of course, that's not the story we have in the Bible, but a different passage in Matthew might answer our question: "For what will it profit a man if he gains the whole world and forfeits his soul? Or what shall a man give in return for his soul?" (Matthew 16:26, ESV).

While the actual parable in Matthew 25 does not endorse wild speculation, it does teach us that we are to do the best we can with what the Master has given us to manage. So it follows that stewardship assumes the responsibility to earn a good return. On performance, Rusty Leonard said:

> I try not to judge people on that....First of all, there is no such thing as a pure portfolio—there is no sinless person, no sinless company. There is always an element of sin in any company. So there is this tension between having a stewardship responsibility to honor the Lord with your money by making sure the things you're investing in are not undermining what the Lord is trying to accomplish, and also a stewardship responsibility to get the best return.[60]

Tension doesn't always exist between earning a positive return and being intentional about how we pursue it. But when it does, different people will come to different answers on how to reconcile the tension. It's important not to judge others on where they come down on balancing that equation. In Rusty's words, "You would hope there are some who would put significant emphasis or at least equal weight to [values-screening] as much as the returns."

Myth #3: There Aren't Enough Options

One exciting development I have observed in BRI, especially over the past five years, is an increasing number of BRI managers and funds from which to choose. The talent pool of managers offering BRI is steadily increasing, spurring healthy competition and attracting more assets as a whole. As of the time of this writing, several BRI funds have achieved four-star and five-star rankings on Morningstar*, outpacing their non-screened peers. But keep in mind that the purpose of this book is not to recommend specific investment funds. Morningstar[16] rankings can be fickle, and top-performing managers (whether BRI-screened or not) may drift in and out of favor on Morningstar* at different times. It's important not to chase performance exclusively when selecting *any* investment, so this principle certainly applies in the selection of BRI funds.

My point is that the number of talented BRI managers is expanding, and a competent financial advisor will know what attributes to look for, beyond the Morningstar* ranking, to implement a BRI approach with excellence. We encourage you to work with a competent financial advisor who is knowledgeable about BRI, and who is free of any conflicting constraints or agendas.

MYTH #4: IT COSTS MORE

This is a quasi-myth. It is true that some investment choices may carry a higher cost, primarily because of the additional layer of due diligence required to run the screens and subscribe to BRI databases. As any start-up entrepreneur will tell you, there is a difference between adding expense, and adding value. Seasoned shoppers know that the lowest-priced item is not always the best value. It all depends on the quality of the merchandise. Suppose it did cost us something extra to implement BRI. Thinking like an entrepreneur, what is the value to *you* of having your

---

*The overall Morningstar Rating for a fund is derived from a weighted average of the performance figures associated with its three-, five-, and ten-year (if applicable) Morningstar Ratings metrics. For each fund with at least a three-year history, Morningstar calculates a Morningstar Rating based on a Morningstar Risk-Adjusted Return measure that accounts for variations in a fund's monthly performance (including the effects of sales charges, loads, and redemption fees), placing more emphasis on downward variations and rewarding consistent performance.

portfolio aligned to your faith and values, as you've aligned other areas of your life? Is it worth an extra 1 percent? That's a question we must each answer for ourselves.

Some might say, "Well, I can get a low-cost mutual fund at an annual expense of 0.20 percent, so why would I invest in a fund that charges an extra 1.0 percent for screening?" The more important question is not, "What are the net expenses?" but rather, "What are the net returns after all fees?" Net return is ultimately how we measure the bottom line. One of the reasons some fund companies are able to maintain such a low expense is because they are passively managed. Passively managed funds are programmed to invest in a way that replicates a benchmark index, such as the S&P 500 Index, without any active management. Since most BRI funds currently available are actively managed, this is not really an apples-to-apples comparison. For now, none of the passive indexes published include the BRI screens (a topic we will address further in the next chapter). Still, as more investment dollars flow toward BRI and develop economies of scale, these added costs will continue to decrease.

MYTH #5: A MEANS TO AN END

There are some who believe it doesn't matter how we earn and invest money, so long as we are generous with the profits. But for the Christ follower, the end never justifies the means. Deuteronomy 23:18 says, "You must not bring the earnings of a...prostitute into the house of the LORD your God to pay any vow." When Judas felt remorse for his betrayal and tried to return the silver, even the Pharisees recognized the incongruity of accepting blood money into the temple (Matthew 27:3–6). This is not to say that earnings for giving must come from God-honoring sources, while earnings earmarked for, say, family needs can come from any source. Remember, God owns all of our wealth—even our very selves—and none of a committed Christian's spending, saving, or giving *ends* can be used to justify immoral *means*.

It's also important not to succumb to legalistic or self-righteous attitudes about investing or giving, believing we earn salvation or spiritual status by righteous actions. In the end, neither giving decisions nor investment decisions are the basis for our faith. They're simply an outward expression of what God has already done in our hearts. For the Christ follower who is seeking to be generous with money in response to God's love and sacrifice, BRI presents an alignment opportunity also, to think about how we invest and earn money.

MYTH #6: IT'S TOO HARD, SO WHY BOTHER?

As consumers, we can't always know what companies we are helping when we choose one brand over another. Sometimes we do know, and with that knowledge comes increased responsibility. For example, if you heard on the news that a certain brand of jeans was utilizing child slave labor in the developing world, chances are you would stop buying their jeans. You might even go so far as to throw away pairs you already owned and encourage your friends to do the same. But most of the time, we just don't know.

However, knowing is now becoming easier. As a result of BRI's screening databases and ongoing research, now we do know the truth for a vast majority of publicly traded companies. BRI provides an opportunity to increase our knowledge and awareness of corporate practices, and then make informed investment decisions. There's no longer any reason to remain ignorant. BRI has made alignment to faith and values readily available to every investor.

We also need not be sedated into inaction by the notion that BRI is not 100-percent pure. BRI is a matter of the heart, not a legalistic requirement. As we've already noted, there is no such thing as a sinless company in which to invest. My friend Bill Robinson said, "If you drill down far enough you are going to hit dirt." There are elements of sin in every business enterprise, because every business is run by imperfect human beings. Our relationships (remember the First Story of the House) and spending choices (Second Story) will never fully reflect the perfect love of Jesus Christ either, but we do the best we can. We strive to love our neighbor, comfort those who are mourning, and feed the poor the best that we know how. We do what we can, imperfectly, with joy in response to the perfect love God has shown us. BRI is an opportunity to extend that worshipful response to another area of life—our investments—by drawing a line between companies that obviously violate biblical values and all the rest.

We may screen out the alcohol company selling cheap beer to minors, but maybe not the industrial manufacturer supplying rolled aluminum to make the cans. We may stop direct corporate donations to the largest abortion provider in the country, but still own a soap company that fills the bathroom dispensers in a Planned Parenthood office. These are examples of how interconnected our free-market economy has become. The BRI screens will never be perfect, but the screening is worthwhile. Just as hunger will never be eradicated until the return of Christ, it is still worthwhile to support soup kitchens and to stop and help the tearful woman in rags on the street corner. We do the best we can, out of love and compassion, with the tools and resources we've been given. All of our pursuits will contain flaws, but as G.K. Chesterton once noted, "If a thing is worth doing, it is worth doing badly."

Myth-Busting Wrap-Up

As you consider the myths surrounding BRI we've addressed in this chapter, ask yourself, *What has been my experience when I talk with other Christian believers about BRI? What stereotypes and assumptions do people make about BRI? How would I now evaluate BRI as a viable approach to God-honoring investing?*

And don't forget this book's simple call to action: search the Scriptures in prayer, talk with your pastor and financial advisor about the opportunity for alignment that BRI presents, and be faithful to what God is teaching you in this area.

6. BACK TO VALUES:
A HISTORICAL PERSPECTIVE

> We all want progress, but if you're on the wrong road,
> progress means doing an about-turn and walking back
> to the right road; in that case, the man who turns back
> soonest is the most progressive.
>
> C.S. LEWIS

Taking a long view, the concept of the American corporation
and free-market trading of capital (that is, stocks) has only been
around for about four hundred years.[61] Just like any other form
of business ownership, stocks represent part-ownership in a
company that provides real goods and services to the marketplace. This concept hit home for me after reading an article in
Christianity Today, "Christ's Returns," by Mary (Naber) King,
which was originally published in 2001.[62] King graduated cum
laude from Harvard in 1998 with a degree in economics and the
comparative study of religion. Her article referenced a long history of leaders taking a moral stance on business practices. For
example, in 1524 Martin Luther famously said:

> Among themselves the merchants have a common rule
> which is their chief maxim…I care nothing about my
> neighbor; so long as I have my profit and satisfy my
> greed, of what concern is it to me if it injures my neigh-
> bor in ten ways at once? There you see how shamelessly
> this maxim flies squarely in the face not only of Chris-
> tian love but also of natural law.[63]

Of course, ethics in business goes back much further than
four hundred years. In the Old Testament, Leviticus 19:11 (ESV)

reads, "You shall not steal; you shall not deal falsely; you shall not lie to one another." This, by the way, is a direct quote from God, which Moses recorded in the Bible's third book following his encounter on Mount Sinai. King Solomon, who lived during the tenth century BC, wisely noted in Proverbs 10:2 (ESV), "Treasures gained by wickedness do not profit, but righteousness delivers from death."

Other historical examples highlighted in Mary King's article include businessman John Woolman, who in the seventeenth century refused to purchase cotton or dye supplies handled by slaves, as well as Philadelphia's Religious Society of Friends (Quakers), who resolved not to deal in the slave trade. John Wesley (1703–1791) is another well-known theologian in history, whose sermon titled "The Use of Money" outlined basic tenets of social investing. In Wesley's words, "We ought to gain all we can gain but this it is certain we ought not to do; we ought not to gain money at the expense of life, nor at the expense of our health."[64] These examples in history illustrate how a person of faith should align methods of business and profit earning with his or her faith.

THE RISE OF THE MODERN CORPORATION

Over the centuries, human nature has not changed. But other things have. Political structures have developed to allow the greatest experiment in democracy and free markets—the United States—to thrive. Today, US corporations have amassed so much capital that many of the Fortune 500 companies have budgets larger than some countries and, thanks to globalization, an international presence that rivals many state departments. Large corporations in today's global economy wield tremendous power in terms of allocation of capital resources. Only in the last twenty years or so have some corporations chosen to exercise that power by engaging in controversial political and social issues unrelated to their products or services, using shareholder resources in an effort to shape and influence culture.

Ironically, aligning investment dollars with values used to be a lot easier in eras when individual investors had a more direct connection to the stocks they owned. It used to be that if you became a shareholder, you received an official stock certificate printed on fine paper evidencing your bona fide ownership, encouraging an emotional connection to the company. Think of a classic American retail department store. As a part-owner in the company, you may then have been more inclined to pay attention to the cleanliness of the stores, or to notice when someone walked down the street with shopping bags from a competing store. Nowadays, when you buy stocks, your ownership is recorded electronically and stock certificates have become more or less a novelty item.

The Rise of Mutual Funds

Mutual funds—a form of pooling resources for investment purposes—were first introduced in America at the turn of the twentieth century, offering the common investor access to capital markets once privy only to an exclusive circle. But, as a result of the Great Depression, the world wars, and a slow market recovery, mutual funds did not reach critical mass in terms of popularity with Main Street investors until around forty years ago. (The financial markets did not fully recover to their 1929 peak until 1954.) Since then, mutual funds have taken off in popularity and have increased market participation dramatically.

But in the process, mutual funds have also created a layer of separation between the ultimate recipient of capital (the publicly-traded corporation) and the steward (the investor). In many ways, a mutual fund is like a black box where you put investment dollars in and hope that profits come out. Investors in mutual funds may understand that they have their money in a "large growth" fund, but as to the individual companies, who knows? In reality, the name of the mutual fund is just the outer wrapper. When you invest in a mutual fund, you are actually purchasing an ownership stake in the basket of companies in which that mutual fund invests.

You can get a fund's top-ten holdings report fairly easily on the web, or scour SEC filings for published reports, but a complete list of a specific mutual fund's holdings is not information readily at the fingertips of the average investor. And even if you do find a complete list of all the companies a mutual fund holds, you have no control over which companies those are. You take them or leave them all with the fund.

To further distance investors from the end use of their capital, a relatively new investment philosophy known as "technical analysis" has also become popular in the past decade. Technical analysts are essentially trend followers who have reduced stocks to nothing more than charts and lines on a screen, and have no interest whatsoever in the underlying companies.

RECONSTRUCTING THE THIRD STORY

In the past two decades, various groups have taken steps to bridge this gap between the investor and the corporation, using tools that allow investors to peek inside the black box and reconnect their investment capital with their values. BRI was really borne out of the concept of Socially Responsible Investing (SRI), which emerged in the 1970s and has gained traction in the last twenty years or so. In many ways, BRI and SRI are closely related to each other. The diagram below demonstrates the similarities and differences between the two approaches to screening investments:

Comparison of BRI and SRI

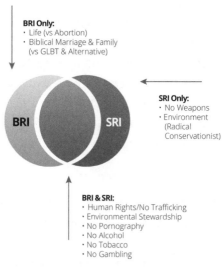

BRI Only:
- Life (vs Abortion)
- Biblical Marriage & Family (vs GLBT & Alternative)

BRI

SRI

SRI Only:
- No Weapons
- Environment (Radical Conservationist)

BRI & SRI:
- Human Rights/No Trafficking
- Environmental Stewardship
- No Pornography
- No Alcohol
- No Tobacco
- No Gambling

Naturally, BRI adds some issues that SRI does not address, because its screens are based on biblical principles rather than on prevailing social attitudes. It's interesting, however, that many of the biblically-based screens have also been identified by SRI as harmful to society, resulting in the overlap (the shared screening issues) illustrated in the diagram. For this reason, BRI and faith-based investing are generally considered to be a subset under the broad umbrella of "socially responsible" investment options. According to a study published in 2010 by the Social Investment Forum, over 10 percent of the total world's capital, or an estimated $3.1 trillion dollars, is invested in a socially responsible manner.

While BRI has been around for roughly half the time SRI has and still represents a very small fraction of total SRI investments, BRI is growing rapidly. In November 2012, Morningstar published an article titled "Getting Religion with Faith-Based

Mutual Funds" by David Kathman, CFA. The article described the increasing availability of faith-based funds for investors with strong religious beliefs, and how this subcategory of socially responsible investing has matured significantly from five years ago. With more than thirty billion dollars in assets attributable to faith-based funds as of October 2012, Kathman wrote, "Enough has changed that it's worth taking a fresh look."[65]
BRI continues to attract attention. As recently as November 2013, the Wall Street Journal featured an article on BRI and faith-based investing, citing that "some investors are finding meaning by putting their money where their faith is."[66]

A LESSON FROM ISLAM

One example of faith-based investing in the marketplace is the development of the Russell-Jadwa Shariah Index*. In a 2009 joint venture with Jadwa, Russell created a market index based on Shariah law. According to the *Encyclopedia Britannica,* the

---

*The Russell-Jadwa Shariah Index offers an accurate and complete global-equity market index that reflects established Shariah investment guidelines. Combining the deep experience of the Russell Indexes and the oversight of Jadwa Investment, these indexes are the best-available representation of the global Shariah compliant opportunity set. Based on the broad and deep Russell Global Index universe, specific-sector and financial-based filters are applied to ensure the exclusion of noncompliant companies, according to Shariah law. After going through the screening process, the result is a series of indexes which reflects the best possible subset of the global market for Shariah compliant investors. The Russell Global Index measures the performance of the global equity market based on all investable equity securities. All securities in the Russell Global Index are classified according to size, region, country, and sector. As a result the Index can be segmented into thousands of distinct benchmarks.

†Any reference to Northwestern Mutual Life Insurance Co. is for illustrative purposes only in connection to historical, factual events and does not constitute a recommendation to buy or sell any security. See also important disclosures.

††The Standard & Poor's 500 Index (S&P 500) is a capitalization-weighted index of 500 stocks designed to measure performance of the broad domestic economy through changes in the aggregate market value of 500 stocks representing all major industries. The S&P 500 is an unmanaged index which cannot be invested into directly.

word *Sharīah,* also spelled *Sharia,* is the fundamental religious concept of Islam, namely its law, systematized during the second and third centuries of the Muslim era (eighth to ninth centuries AD).[67]

To provide context, Russell Investments is a global investment company headquartered in Tacoma, Washington, with over one hundred billion dollars in assets under management, serving individual and institutional clients in more than forty countries. Russell also happens to be a wholly-owned subsidiary of Northwestern Mutual Life Insurance Company†.[68] Jadwa is a Saudi company regulated by the Saudi Arabian Capital Markets Authority and offers a range of Shariah-compliant investment services.[69]

For the average investor, the most widely recognized index in the US is probably either the Standard & Poor's 500†† or the Dow Jones Industrial Average*. The "S&P" and "the Dow," as they are commonly known, are routinely displayed on the national evening news and in the business section of newspapers to provide us with a sense for how the market is doing. But in the institutional world, the most closely followed indexes have been the Russell Global Indexes†, because Russell indexes are typically used as a benchmark for comparing performance of money managers against their peers. To put things in perspective, Russell

---

* The Dow Jones Industrial Average (Dow) is comprised of 30 stocks that are major factors in their industries and widely held by individuals and institutional investors. The Dow is an unmanaged index which cannot be invested into directly.

† The Russell Global Indexes are a family of indexes constructed to provide a comprehensive and unbiased barometer for the global segment and are completely reconstituted annually to accurately reflect changes in the market over time. The Russell Global Indexes are unmanaged indexes which cannot be invested into directly.

All indexes are unmanaged and cannot be invested into directly. Unmanaged index returns do not reflect fees, expenses, or sales charges. Index performance is not indicative of the performance of any investment. Past performance is no guarantee of future results.

US Indexes have over 3.9 *trillion* dollars in assets benchmarked to them.

Interestingly, the Shariah screens are very much compatible with the BRI screens on most moral issues, with some differences. For example, one difference is that Shariah law does not permit the collection and payment of interest (which rules out most banks). It may seem a bit surprising that an American company like Russell, with so much global influence, would create a Shariah-values-compliant index, but not a BRI-compliant index. After all, according to Barna Research, more than four out of five Americans claim to be Christian and half as many can be classified as born-again Christians. Nine out of ten American adults own a Bible, most adults read the Bible during the year, and a huge majority claim they know all of the basic teachings of the Bible.[70] And yet, in America there is no BRI stock index.

To be fair, Russell is not favoring one belief system over another. This is a very important point. After all, America is the greatest political experiment in economic, religious, and political freedom the world has ever seen. Russell is simply responding to what their customers in the Islamic community expressed as a need, and their customers were willing to pay Russell to do it. If a multibillion-dollar Christian foundation or an individual investor with similar means felt strongly enough about tracking their accounts against a BRI index, and were willing to pay for it, I have no doubt that Russell or another Wall Street firm would be willing to build it.

> And I heard the voice of the Lord saying, "Whom shall I send, and who will go for us?" Then I said, "Here am I! Send me."
>
> ISAIAH 6:8, ESV

Rusty Leonard expressed one disappointment to me: Christian leadership in the church has largely ignored the opportunity BRI presents. "It's frustrating because it is not being ignored by Islamic leadership or by secular leadership. They are very much active in trying to convince people in their religious or environmental groups, respectively, to invest in a way that reflects their beliefs. Among the Christian community, [BRI proponents] are pretty lonely voices out there."

What the Church Needs

In the fall of 2012, I participated in a BRI conference call with Randy Alcorn, author and founder of Eternal Perspectives Ministries. One of the participants asked Randy, "Why have Christian leaders largely ignored BRI when secular leaders have embraced SRI and changed culture with the 'Going-Green' movement?"

Randy answered, "It is partly sin, and partly that pastors may feel that they are venturing into an area they are not knowledgeable about. Most pastors do not have formal training in investing or finance, so they don't feel comfortable answering that question." Randy went on to say, "The church needs clear communication tools, as well as financial advisors who are willing to assist investors in implementing BRI."

At the time of the conference call, this book was about 75-percent complete, and when I heard him say that I nearly leaped out of my chair in excitement. My hope is that this book helps meet that need.

7. DEMAND SUPPLY!

In matters of style, swim with the current; in matters of
principle, stand like a rock."

THOMAS JEFFERSON

Sometimes I think the bottleneck hindering BRI from taking off
is not Main Street investors, but rather Wall Street advisors. The
demand is there, but it's a hidden demand because the Christian
investing public doesn't realize it's an option. In Spokane, there's
a restaurant chain called The Onion that is famous for their
deep-fried Oreos. As amazing as these treats are, they are off-
the-menu. You have to know about them and ask for them.
When I first visited the city, my wife (at the time we were still
dating) said deep-fried Oreos were something I had to experience for myself. I'm not really sure why the item is not listed on
the menu. Perhaps the restaurant wants to look good on paper
for the American Heart Association. The point is that for the
unsuspecting tourist, deep-fried Oreos simply do not exist. In
Los Angeles it's considered Hollywood chic to order something
not on the menu. Most people, on the other hand, look at a
restaurant's menu and make their selection based on the choices
available.

An old saying goes, "You don't know what you don't know."
That's why I think BRI has such potential. The reason most
Christian investors are not asking for BRI is simply because they
don't know it exists. Or when they do learn about BRI, their
financial advisor discourages them from taking it seriously. Ron
Blue shared with me, "I think there are believers, people who
would be counseled and led [toward BRI], but the advisors are
afraid of it."

Famous American psychologist Abraham Maslow once

noted, "If you only have a hammer, you tend to see every problem as a nail."[71] Wall Street can be like that. I know; I've been there! In 2004, I had an encounter with a friend who needed investment advice. Back then, I was relatively new to the securities industry and eager to establish client relationships. We were meeting because I proposed he consider the management firm where I worked, which was putting up great numbers at the time. My friend had also been talking to someone at our church about faith-based investing, and was considering going that direction. Over lunch at a trendy little bistro in Santa Monica, I probably spent an hour explaining to my friend how faith-based investing was imperfect and too hard to implement, and therefore not worth trying. He ended up going with the faith-based approach, and I respected his decision.

At the time, I was genuinely advocating what I believed was in my friend's best interest. I believed in the firm where I worked and that we could help him. It happened that we did not offer a faith-based approach. When you go through sales training at a company and are surrounded by all the company's marketing materials, you have a natural tendency to believe your company's products are the best solution. Financial advisors may not even be aware they're being swayed toward or away from certain options; the company bias effect is subtle yet powerful.

Looking back, I'm humbled at how my own investment philosophy has evolved since then. Now, when I talk to pastors and church leaders about BRI and they see my enthusiasm, their eyes light up. A common reaction I hear is, "Wow, I didn't know you could do that!" And this is a full ten years after Mary King's article, mentioned in the previous chapter, first appeared in *Christianity Today*. The demand is there, and Wall Street firms will eventually have to begin expanding their toolbox in order to stay competitive. One such firm is the Aris Corporation.

Keith Weir, senior vice president and managing director of Aris, described in an interview how the company was formed in 1974 primarily as a retirement-services firm. The company reorganized in the early 2000s and the executive leadership, many of whom are strong Christians, decided to leverage the firm's thirty-plus years of institutional investment experience to build high-quality BRI and faith-based portfolios. While the BRI portfolios represent a small percentage of the over one billion dollars in assets under their management, Aris Corporation is now seeing rapid growth within this segment of investors. Keith went on to share that by introducing a variety of different screening options, including BRI, "Aris is using a 'big tent' approach to get more people involved in the area of values-based investing." When I asked why more firms weren't following suit, Keith said, "Personally, I believe there is a lack of communication to the general marketplace, because financial advisors have been reluctant to introduce BRI to their clients. We think this market will grow tremendously in the years ahead."

Sometimes I think the bottleneck hindering BRI from taking off is not Main Street investors, but rather Wall Street advisors.

Around Christmas of 2010, I received as a gift a copy of the book *Kingdom Gains,* by Dwight Short. The book is a great resource for financial advisors and may be used as a guide for further understanding BRI on a technical level. As I mentioned earlier, Dwight recently retired from Merrill Lynch[21] after successfully building a practice that managed over six hundred million dollars in client assets. I asked Dwight what had inspired the book, and he said, "It was something I felt God calling me to do. BRI is such a great idea. I had incorporated it late in my career at Merrill Lynch*, and I wanted to try and leave a legacy for other advisors to start doing it long before their final ten years—even immediately—if they felt so inclined."

When I asked where he thought BRI was going in the future, Dwight responded, "I believe BRI is a tremendous movement that is just barely getting traction now." I agree. Kingdom Advisors recently announced that in 2012, the Financial Industry Regulatory Authority (FINRA), the largest independent regulator for all securities firms doing business in the United States, recognized the Qualified Kingdom Advisor™ credential as a valid designation issued by Kingdom Advisors.[†72] This designation is fast becoming the standard of excellence with the Christian investing public.

Additionally, many Wall Street and independent firms are beginning to acknowledge that the Christian market segment has unique planning needs and are beginning to support advisors desiring to serve this market. It's an exciting time, as I see more and more advisors helping individuals and families practice biblical stewardship, and helping them experience freedom from economic fear, bondage, and conflict.

I asked Dwight about his experience at Merrill Lynch*, and he shared that the firm has been supportive of Kingdom Advisors in recent years. "It wasn't always that way, but that is changing." Dwight believes other firms will also begin recognizing Christian believers as a valid and attractive market segment. "I don't think there's any question. If you want to stay competitive, firms are going to have to have some way of competing and keeping a focus on the Christian investor."

---

*Any reference to Merrill Lynch is for illustrative purposes only in connection to historical, factual events and does not constitute a recommendation to buy or sell any security. See also important disclosures.

†Note that FINRA does not endorse any professional designation.

It is an important step to acknowledge that Christian believers have a place at the table when talking about diversity and different cultural perspectives.

There's also been a significant development at Ameriprise Financial*, an independent broker/dealer and financial services firm. Ameriprise Financial created a Christian Franchise Advisor Network and a Christian Employee Network to serve as resources to their Christian client and employee communities, respectively.[73] To be fair, Christianity is just one of many focus groups to which Ameriprise is catering as part of a broader diversity campaign. Other groups include the gay and lesbian communities. This is an important, even historic, step: the acknowledgment that Christian believers have a place at the table when talking about diversity and different cultural perspectives. Dwight Short explains: "It began with an energy and interest among the individual advisors at Ameriprise. And once that was recognized to be a very serious thing, and the firm's leadership got on board to make it a high priority, there has now been an official acknowledgment of the Christian investor marketplace. And I think that will spread. I think you'll see that happen at a lot of other firms eventually."

If you want to stay competitive, firms are going to have to have some way of competing and keeping a focus on the Christian investor.

DWIGHT SHORT

---

*Any reference to Ameriprise Financial is for illustrative purposes only in connection to historical, factual events and does not constitute a recommendation to buy or sell any security. See also important disclosures.

Another resource that recently came online is the Christian Investment Forum, a nonprofit website Dwight helped orchestrate in a joint effort with six other sponsor companies. The purpose was to create an objective gathering place for information about BRI, and the Christian Investment Forum is quickly becoming a kind of trade association for BRI. Dwight shared, "We wanted a place where people can go and see all kinds of different approaches. And one of the things the website is attempting to do is to be 'a very large tent.' We have a white paper that we've issued that clearly calls for people to understand that we're doing this for Christians and on behalf of Christians, and anyone can come to the website and find it *easily*. If a Jewish person or Muslim person works as a financial advisor and has Christian clients, we want this website to be a place where they can go and understand the positions that we're taking, and the positions that we feel need to be explained to others that are part of the marketplace."

What's most unique about the website is that it's the first objective landing page providing information about BRI that is not controlled by any one vendor or provider. While the website offers sponsorships to companies that would like to help support the costs of the service, the site does not endorse any particular way of implementing BRI. The website also hopes to be a place where advisors, investors, vendors, and investment managers in the BRI space can come together and have meaningful dialogue. You can find more information about the Christian Investment Forum website in the Appendix, "Additional Resources," at the end of this book.

THE NEXT GENERATION OF STEWARDS

Also, generational shifts are taking place that will affect how investors participate in capital markets. I currently have the privilege of serving as a corporate board member for the YMCA of the Inland Northwest, and a few years ago the board had a retreat to develop our YMCA's next Five-Year Strategic Plan. The CEO brought in an outside consultant and we gathered a lot of research about families and generational trends. What we discovered was that the next generation, referred to as "Generation-Y" or "Millennials," is to a great extent cause-driven. They are deeply concerned about impact and the need to make a difference in our world. Millennials are also highly mobilized through social media. It wasn't until I struggled to understand the purpose of Twitter that I realized I am not so young anymore. The next generation gets it. Social media is not about the cliché "guess what I ate for breakfast" anymore. It's about getting the word out and helping people make a difference in the world.

We are about to experience, over the next twenty years, the largest generational shift of wealth in human history, as Tom Brokaw's "Greatest Generation" transfers literally *trillions* of dollars to Boomers, Gen-X, and Millennials. Considering the Millennials' tendency to want to make a positive difference, I believe they will have a tremendous impact on how capital is deployed once this generational shift in wealth occurs. In the future, I believe values-based investing will be the norm. Perhaps one of the many financial news and research websites will come up with some clever visual rating system for integrating SRI and BRI databases to measure where a company falls on the values-based landscape.

I described this vision to Bill Robinson, concluding, "That's the future."

Bill replied, "I think you're right."

How will we get there? It all starts with you, the client. Begin by asking your financial advisor. Wall Street firms tend to listen to their advisors, and advisors tend to listen to their clients. If

Wall Street senses a need in the marketplace, they will listen because they are a sales-driven industry.

> It all starts with you, the client. Begin by asking your financial advisor. Wall Street firms tend to listen to their advisors, and advisors tend to listen to their clients.

What's interesting is that BRI has now been accepted in the big firms. Human beings are social animals, and most find it uncomfortable to stray too far ahead of the pack with new ideas. This is part of our emotional constitution. Fortunately, you no longer have to be an "early adopter" to embrace BRI.

BRI has made great strides in the past ten years, and I expect that momentum will only accelerate in the next ten years. The demand is there.

8. COLLECTIVE IMPACT

> "Truly, I say to you, if you have faith like a grain of mustard seed, you will say to this mountain, 'Move from here to there,' and it will move, and nothing will be impossible for you."
>
> MATTHEW 17:20, ESV

Through BRI, an individual has the opportunity to align his or her investment decisions to their faith and biblical values. But BRI has the potential to impact more than just the individual investor; it also presents the opportunity to impact culture. For a recent historical example of the way ethics and investing can influence culture, we need look no further than the efforts of one man, Leon Sullivan (1922–2001), and the Sullivan Principles in the 1970s–1990s. In an article published by our local newspaper, the *Spokesman Review,* I discussed a brief history of the way Sullivan contributed to the end of apartheid by illuminating corporate behavior in Africa and mobilizing institutional investors:

> In 1977, the Rev. Leon Sullivan (at the time a board member for General Motors) drafted a code of conduct for practicing business in South Africa which led to the discovery that many U.S. companies were not addressing discrimination within South Africa. Soon thereafter, cities, states, colleges, faith-based groups and pension funds throughout the United States quickly began divesting from companies operating in South Africa, creating economic and political pressure that ultimately contributed to the end of apartheid.[74]

Sullivan made the connection between ethics and financial investment. At the time, General Motors* was one of the largest corporations in the US and a major employer in South Africa.

In commemoration of his life and work, *Christianity Today* wrote, "The Sullivan Principles enshrined a set of corporate practices that boldly challenged the apartheid system then in force by calling for racial desegregation in the workplace—including in cafeterias and toilets—equal pay for equal work, the promotion of more non-whites to better positions, and improved housing, schooling, recreation and health facilities for workers."[75] In Sullivan's own words back then, "There is no greater moral issue in the world today than apartheid. Apartheid is against the will of God and humanity."[76]

Just as the Sullivan Principles inspired a movement that contributed to the end of apartheid, the advent of BRI has resulted in a growing movement of investors motivated by biblical principles, acting in concert to exert pressure on the business community for positive moral change. As more investors make that choice, corporations will eventually notice. That's part of the beauty of free markets.

One individual who has made it his life mission to engage corporate culture head-on is Thomas Strobhar of ProVita Advisors in Colorado. While Strobhar's approach takes a different tack than the collective opportunity represented by BRI investing, his story is remarkable and serves to prove that it's entirely possible to make a positive impact. Corporations *are* listening.

In a recent phone conversation, Strobhar shared with me, "I think moral investing is important, but it's just a starting point. The real purpose of all this is to try to slow, stop things like abor-

---

*Any reference to General Motors Corp. is for illustrative purposes only in connection to historical, factual events and does not constitute a recommendation to buy or sell any security. See also important disclosures.

tion, pornography, same-sex marriage. Most people feel they've come to some alignment of their Christian values. To me, BRI is important—but it's a starting point."

Strobhar grew up across the street from a partial-birth abortion clinic in the 1980s, and while he would sometimes picket there, he wondered how he could use his professional skills to better deter abortion. Then in July 1989, Strobhar saw an article in *BusinessWeek* titled "Something Planned Parenthood Didn't Plan." The article reported how the Pillsbury Company*—at the time one of the world's largest producers of grain and other foodstuffs—had given money to Planned Parenthood and received five thousand nasty letters in response. Generally, corporate donations are supposed to make people feel good about the company and create goodwill, but here was a case where the Planned Parenthood donation was actually creating ill will.

This realization prompted Strobhar to found Pro Vita Advisors, a nonprofit organization dedicated to exposing and confronting the business aspects of abortion. "I saw that people didn't like Pillsbury giving money to Planned Parenthood, and I thought that might be a breach of their 'fiduciary responsibility.' Now that's a legal term, but it's an important legal term." Strobhar went out and purchased a small amount of stock in about thirty different companies that had given money to Planned Parenthood, and as a shareholder he wrote letters to the chairman of the board of each. Strobhar understood that as owners of the company, shareholders have certain legal rights.

The board of directors of every publicly traded company are charged with the responsibility of doing everything in their power to enhance shareholder value, or in other words, to make money

---

*Any reference to the Pillsbury Company is for illustrative purposes only in connection to historical, factual events and does not constitute a recommendation to buy or sell any security. See also important disclosures.

for the company. This requires that the company's board and its executives act prudently for the benefit of the shareholders. In his letter, Strobhar referenced Planned Parenthood's racist and eugenics past, and how they are the largest abortion-performing organization in the country. The letter referenced the board's fiduciary responsibilities and how they should be sensitive to the fact that these kinds of donations could offend some people and harm the interests of the company's shareholders, who are ultimately the owners.

Most responses to his letter were cold and explained that the company believed they were donating the funds for things like teen sex education or community health services, not for abortion. Then about six months later, Strobhar received a letter from AT&T* informing him they would no longer donate to Planned Parenthood. The next day, AT&T put out a press release to the same effect, ending a twenty-five-year-old tradition of giving fifty thousand dollars per year to Planned Parenthood.

What did Planned Parenthood do? According to Strobhar, "They went absolutely crazy." Planned Parenthood took out full-page ads in the *New York Times*, *Washington Post*, *LA Times*, and other major newspapers across the country. The ad read, "Caving into Extremists, AT&T Hangs Up on Planned Parenthood." In total, Planned Parenthood spent at least five hundred thousand dollars in advertising trying to change AT&T's decision—to no avail. AT&T never gave money to Planned Parenthood again.

Why did Planned Parenthood react so strongly? Strobhar felt that two forces were at work here. First, fifty thousand dollars a year is a lot of money. To put it in perspective, you would need a pot of one million dollars earning 5 percent interest to generate that kind of annual income. But even more significant, AT&T's

---

*Any reference to AT&T is for illustrative purposes only in connection to historical, factual events and does not constitute a recommendation to buy or sell any security. See also important disclosures.

withdrawal represented a loss of prestige for Planned Parenthood, which was far more valuable than the individual donation. It set a precedent for other contributors to recognize that Planned Parenthood is a controversial organization, and Planned Parenthood's fears were well-founded. Shortly afterward, other major US companies including General Mills, Target, and American Express[*], began defunding Planned Parenthood, although much more quietly and without any press releases.[77]

More recently, as the chairman of Life Decisions International, Strobhar has played a key role along with its president, Doug Scott, in getting approximately three hundred companies to stop giving money to Planned Parenthood, leading to losses for Planned Parenthood in the tens of millions of dollars. How did just two individuals accomplish this? In Strobhar's words, "I attended annual meetings. I'd get out there and talk to corporations, address some influential people, and we try to bring up issues that people can change."

I find it interesting that many of these companies saw no problem making donations to controversial organizations like Planned Parenthood as long as no one who cared was really paying attention. The tipping point where companies stop donating to Planned Parenthood seems to occur when more people are upset than pleased by it. It's about simply shining light in dark places.

Most recently, Strobhar has turned his attention to corporations that proactively endorse or support same-sex marriage. Starbucks[†] is one example. In response to Strobhar's comments

---

[*]Any reference to General Mills, Target, or American Express is for illustrative purposes only in connection to historical, factual events and does not constitute a recommendation to buy or sell any security. See also important disclosures.

[†]Any reference to Starbucks is for illustrative purposes only in connection to historical, factual events and does not constitute a recommendation to buy or sell any security. See also important disclosures.

at the annual shareholder meeting in March 2013, Starbucks CEO Howard Schultz invited investors who disagreed with the company's support of same-sex marriage to sell their shares.[78]

Strobhar says, "It seems most people don't care about the destruction of traditional marriage in this country. Nowadays, if you take a position that marriage should be between one man and one woman, you are labeled a hater and a bigot—which is certainly not the case. I may be many things, but I'm not one of those things."

When I asked how he finds the courage to take stands on these controversial issues, Strobhar replied, "I enjoy that kind of confrontation—most people don't. I guess it's my strength." Strobhar further reflected, "I hope that in some sense it is an expression of my faith, and that's what inspires me. Every time you go to a church, there's typically a cross on the steeple, to remind people of the sacrifice that was made. Because of what Christ did on the cross, I would think that implies on our part a sincere effort commensurate with a sincere faith."

> I have these skills and try to do something more productive than just picketing in front of a clinic. Not to demean picketing; in some ways it's great for the soul.
>
> THOMAS STROBHAR

In this book I'm not suggesting we attend shareholder meetings or file resolutions as Strobhar did. That's not part of this book's call to action. I share Strobhar's story for one reason—to help you imagine what might happen if the entire Christian community of believers simply started paying attention to where their investment dollars were flowing. Companies might think twice about engaging in controversial business practices if the consequences become material enough—that is, if enough investors sell their stock—to affect the company's stock price. As demonstrated by Leon Sullivan in the 1970s, capital is the lifeblood of corporations. If enough investors retreat from a stock, the company will adapt its behavior to stop the bleeding.

> Let us have faith that right makes might, and in that faith, let us, to the end, dare to do our duty as we understand it.

ABRAHAM LINCOLN[79]

THE TROUBLE WITH DONATIONS

We live in a free country, and individuals are free to vote and give their own personal money however they feel politically or morally inclined. That's what makes this country great. We can all coexist and agree to disagree in this free economy of ideas. The trouble with corporate donations is that the corporation's assets, including its cash, technically belong to the pool of investors represented as shareholders. When a company makes a charitable donation, it is giving away money that belongs to the shareholders. The company enters controversial territory when it suggests that it may donate funds in a way that will benefit all shareholders, or in a way that all shareholders will feel good about.

Milton Friedman (1912–2006), the great American economist and recipient of the Nobel Memorial Prize in Economic Sciences, once said, "Charitable contributions are a dubious corporate enterprise. Their only legitimacy resides in an attempt to enhance the business of a company."[80] If an individual wants to write a check to Planned Parenthood to support abortions, they can do that. If the CEO or chairman has an affinity for Planned Parenthood, let him or her write personal checks, not shareholder checks. It's that simple. All BRI is saying is that corporations are the stewards of shareholder money, and many shareholders would have strong moral objections to seeing their investment capital funding Planned Parenthood. Accordingly, it is wise and appropriate for corporations to refrain from making such donations.

Of course, it would be impossible for all shareholders to agree on every corporate action or decision. That's why shareholders elect the board of directors, who in turn appoint executives to run the day-to-day operations. Objections to charitable contributions are not the same, however, as differences that may arise over operational questions such as how to best pursue new product development or marketing strategy. Charitable donations, and especially controversial donations that touch on moral faith issues, draw into question the very purpose of the corporation.

FROM A METHOD OF INVESTING TO A MOVEMENT

Recently I had the privilege to meet Jeff Rogers, recipient of the Larry Burkett Award at the 2013 Kingdom Advisors annual conference. Jeff is also the founder of Stewardship Advisory Group and co-founder of Stewardship Asset Management. Having been shaped by the ministry of Larry Burkett in the 1980s, Jeff has spent his entire career devoted to sharing the message of biblical stewardship. When I asked about his personal story as an early adopter of BRI, Jeff shared this: "To me, Biblically Responsible Investing is simply a natural outflow of my belief that God is the owner and we are His stewards. I learned that early on in my career, through Howard Dayton of Compass—Finances God's Way™ and the late Larry Burkett. If God is the Owner of all our money and investments (and He is), then shouldn't we invest His money in a way that would please Him as the Owner?"

Jeff was careful to point out that "BRI is not the only aspect of stewardship. God is just as concerned with how we spend His money, how generously we give back to Him, and how generously we serve others with it." Remember the Second Story of the stewardship house analogy? Jeff's comments reaffirm how all three Stories of the Three-Story House analogy are interconnected.

> As an advocate for Biblically Responsible Investing in general, my role is to be an inspiration to my team, and to other advisors and managers who are co-laboring with us to transform BRI from a *method* of investing into a *movement* of investing that pleases God.
>
> JEFF ROGERS

Jeff also serves as chief inspiration officer for Stewardship Asset Management, a separate account platform that implements BRI for high-net-worth families. When I expressed curiosity about his title, Jeff responded, "As an advocate for Biblically Responsible Investing in general, my role is to be an inspiration to my team, and also to other advisors and managers who are co-laboring with us to transform BRI from a *method* of investing into a *movement* of investing that pleases God."

THE ROAD AHEAD

How do we get back to a culture centered on Jesus? The first step is for corporations to shift their focus away from values that are not Jesus' values and, if nothing else, to remain neutral on these hot-button issues. Will porn companies go away? No, of course not. In a free market, basic economics teaches that the law of supply and demand will always prevail. If there is demand for goods and services, then someone, somewhere, will supply them. Human nature has not changed, and modern-day pornography is not all that different from the public bath houses of ancient Rome. The fact is we live in a fallen world, so the demand that spawned the Vice Fund will always exist.

The power behind BRI and its potential for collective impact is the opportunity to influence the flow of capital in the marketplace. If a critical mass of investors implemented BRI, for example, large publicly-traded companies may be compelled to manage their subsidiaries and corporate donations in order to avoid triggering a red flag by the BRI databases, and hence prevent a tidal wave of sell orders. Why? The collective market force of millions of individual and institutional BRI investors would have a material effect on a company's stock price if the company violated a BRI screen. In this way, BRI has the potential to become a deterrent, steering corporations to avoid controversial areas. Recall the impact of Leon Sullivan and the Sullivan Principles. I believe God is up to something in history.

> The power behind BRI and its potential for collective impact is the opportunity to influence the flow of capital in the marketplace.

If you are a Christ follower seeking to honor God in every area of life, your immediate incentive for implementing BRI is simply to honor God in one more life arena—to approach investment decisions with the same attitude of faithfulness, obedience, and joy you bring to marriage, family, work, and everything else. This personal benefit is important. But I challenge you to think even bigger. What if you and I and every Christian believer implemented BRI in his or her investment decision making? Imagine the potential for us to collectively influence corporate culture and society!

9. DRAWING CONCLUSIONS

Failure is not fatal, but failure to change might be.

JOHN WOODEN

At the beginning of this book, I introduced an analogy picturing stewardship as a Three-Story House, with each successive Story integral to and building on the others. We first establish the Foundation—specifically that God owns it all, God's perspective is eternal, and God is provider and protector. This is cemented by our faith in Christ and all that doctrinally springs from it.

Then the First Story represents the way we deal with relationships, how we love and treat others.

Building on our love for God and others, we add the Second Story, which deals with the outflow of wealth—how we give, spend money, and model our lifestyles.

Just as we are intentional about our lifestyle decisions and planning for future needs, we can build on that by adding a Third Story defining the ways we invest and earn money—the inflow of wealth.

For the faithful steward, this model provides a blueprint for managing our relationships, our wealth outflow, *and our wealth inflow (including investments)*, in a manner consistent with our faith values.

Soli Deo gloria is a Latin phrase meaning "Glory to God alone." It has been used by artists like Johann Sebastian Bach, George Frideric Handel, and Christoph Graupner to give God credit for their work. As a doctrine, it means essentially that we do everything for God's glory, and to the exclusion of humankind's self-glorification and pride. Christ followers are to be motivated and inspired to enhance God's reputation, not their own.

> Whatever you do, work at it with all your heart, as working for the Lord, not for men, since you know that you will receive an inheritance from the Lord as a reward. It is the Lord Christ you are serving.

> COLOSSIANS 3:23–24

In the two thousand years since the earthly life of Christ, the concept of stewardship has not changed. But capital markets, political systems, social conventions, and technology have all changed, and are constantly evolving. The challenge then is how to live out our Christian faith and manage our resources faithfully in our modern world. Since Christ walked this planet, the Christian business owner has assumed a moral responsibility not to harm their workers or society. Over time, with the advent of stock market trading and the rise in mutual fund accessibility over the past forty years, the layers of separation have multiplied and created distance between the investor and the ultimate recipient of capital, the corporation. BRI seeks to bridge that gap and build a filtering system into the investment process to help investors choose more carefully what products, services, and causes they are actually supporting with their investment dollars.

Imagine if the entire Christian evangelical community in America, representing a diverse patchwork of denominations and traditions, woke up and started paying attention to how their 401(k)s, IRAs, and company pension plans were invested. According to a 2007 Pew Study, over 26 percent of Americans, or eighty-one million people, identified themselves as "born-again evangelical Christians." In a 2006 Barna Study, which used their own list of criteria to determine who would fit that definition, only 8 percent of Americans, or twenty-four million, were categorized as born-again evangelical Christians. By whichever figure you measure, there are a significant number of people with the potential to yield tremendous influence on corporate culture. But even if BRI never gains that momentum, the primary case for BRI is first and foremost an opportunity for personal alignment of one's investments with one's faith. In Dan Hardt's words, "BRI is simply an expression of our love for God. If you and I and everyone else implementing BRI never made a difference in our world, I would still want to do it."

Jesus had a profound way of taking complex decisions and making them simple. Recently I listened to an inspirational sermon by Ron Pyle, a professor at Whitworth University, and I was reminded how Jesus transforms everything He touches. Professor Pyle shed new light for me on Jesus' encounter with Levi the tax collector.

> [Jesus] went out and saw a tax collector named Levi, sitting at the tax booth; and he said to him, "Follow me." And he got up, left everything, and followed him.
>
> LUKE 5:27–28, NRSV

In Pyle's words, Jesus saw Levi with "godly vision." He saw past Levi's title as a tax collector, a role for which Levi's peers despised him. Jesus extended an invitation that was full of grace and that revealed God's character. Perhaps what this sermon brought home to me even more powerfully was Levi's response. Jesus said, "Follow me," and Levi just got up and left everything. I love the picture of Levi as Pyle painted him: "In that moment, Levi said goodbye to the greed, lying to his neighbors, and abuse that were part of his daily life as a tax collector for the Roman Empire, and made a decision to follow Jesus. He also left some good things, like financial security. Levi knew that once he deserted the tax office, he would never be invited back.

It wasn't like he could just go back to fishing like the other disciples. For him, following Jesus required a decision for which there was no exit strategy." At the end of the sermon, Pyle said, "I want to follow Jesus with that kind of abandon—no Plan B, no safeguards, no tentative trial period." Levi was all-in.

In your walk with Jesus, are you all-in?

This is primarily a book about investing, but it touches on the much deeper subject of integrity. Integrity calls us to live a life that is *wholly* in alignment with our values, beliefs, and principles. For the Christ follower, BRI presents an opportunity to align investment decisions with faith values. It is not a legalistic requirement that will influence our eternal destiny, but a way to freely express our love and gratitude in response to the salvation God has already given us.

Yet the faithful steward might ask whether it is really a matter of choice at all. One day, when the Master returns, we will be required to give an account for the resources we managed here on earth. In his book *The Call,* Os Guinness writes, "Calling is the truth that God calls us to himself so decisively that everything we are, everything we do, and everything we have is invested with a special devotion, dynamism, and direction lived out as a response to his summons and service."[81]

As you reflect on your own spiritual journey, I would encourage you to pray and search the Scriptures about the concepts we have explored in this book. Talk about them with your pastor and your financial advisor. Be faithful to what God is teaching you in this area. If your financial advisor is not knowledgeable about BRI, please direct him or her toward informative resources. Supply will always follow demand, and as more investors demand a values-based approach, more Wall Street and independent firms will have no choice but to further develop these services if they want to stay competitive in the future. Firms are starting to recognize that Christians who want financial advice and services from a biblical perspective represent a legitimate and attractive market.

My advice for the church and to the Christian investor is simple: find a financial advisor who is committed to implementing BRI, knowledgeable about the various faith-based investment solutions that are available, and willing to help you select the best approach based on your individual needs and objectives. You will also find resources in the appendix of this book to assist you in your journey.

I hope this book has planted seeds that provide a fresh perspective on biblical stewardship, and that it has challenged you to consider making the process of investing in today's capital markets an extension of your vital act of

> If you work for a Christian nonprofit, a church, or a business run by Christian owners, consider asking senior leadership about adding BRI to the company's retirement plan menu choices.

daily worship. What is the Lord calling you to in this area of BRI? As a faithful manager of the resources entrusted to you, I commend you on your stewardship journey and encourage you to further explore BRI as an opportunity to align every area of life under the Lordship of Jesus Christ. Ultimately, the goal of every believer is to meet our Lord face-to-face one day and hear the words, "Well done, good and faithful servant."[82]

10. SUMMARY OF KEY PRINCIPLES

LAYING THE FOUNDATION

* God owns it all, and we are His stewards.
* God's perspective is eternal; live for the line, not the dot!
* God is our provider and protector.

THE THREE-STORY HOUSE

First Story: How We Manage Relationships

• Love the Lord your God with all your heart and with all your soul and with all your mind.
• Love your neighbor as yourself.

Second Story: How We Use Money (Wealth Outflow)

• Spend less than you earn.
• Avoid the use of debt.
• Maintain liquidity.
• Think long-term.
• Live generously.
• Draw finish lines; predetermine how much is enough.

Third Story: How We Invest and Earn Money (Wealth Inflow)

• Align how you invest and save for the future to your faith and values.
• Avoid investments that do not honor the Lord or that are harmful to society.
• Make investing decisions a voluntary extension of your vital act of worship.

CALL TO ACTION

* Search the Scriptures in prayer.
* Talk with your financial advisor and pastor about BRI.
* Be faithful to what the Lord is calling you to in this area.

NOTE: Explore the resources provided in the appendix of this book; they will aid you along your journey in response to this call to action.

APPENDIX—ADDITIONAL RESOURCES

Other resources that you might find helpful:

- Find a Qualified Kingdom Advisor™: www.kingdomadvisors.org
- Christian Investment Forum: www.christianinvestmentforum.org
- Master Your Money: www.masteryourmoney.com
- Compass—Finances God's Way™: www.compass1.org
- *Investing with Integrity* website:
  www.investingwithintegrity.net

Other great books to add to your reading list:

- *Good Returns,* by George Schwartz *(on BRI)*
- *Profit or Principles,* by Dwight Short *(on BRI)*
- *Surviving Financial Meltdown,* by Ron Blue & Jeremy White
- *Money, Possessions, & Eternity,* by Randy Alcorn
- *Splitting Heirs,* by Ron Blue
- *Your Money Counts,* by Howard Dayton
- *Million Dollar Dime,* by R. Scott Rodin
- *From Success to Significance,* by Lloyd Reeb

ENDNOTES

1. Dr. Charles R. Swindoll, *Great Lives from God's Word* (Nashville: Thomas Nelson, 2006), 125.

2. *American Heritage Dictionary of the English Language.* 5th ed. Boston: Houghton Mifflin, 2011. Also available at http://www.ahdictionary.com/.

3. Gary D. Moore, *Spiritual Investments* (Radnor: Templeton Foundation Press, 1998), 1.

4. Ron Blue and Jeremy White, *Surviving Financial Meltdown: Confident Decisions in an Uncertain World* (Carol Stream: Tyndale House Publishers, 2009), 4-5.

5. "US Debt Clock," US Debt Clock.org, accessed November 8, 2013, http://www.usdebtclock.org.

6. Patrick Johnson, "The Third Conversion," *Generous Giving Research Library*, accessed November 10, 2013, http://library.generousgiving.org/articles/display.asp?id=18 3.

7. Ron Blue, *Master Your Money* (Chicago: Moody Publishers, 2004), 12.

8. Ken Blanchard, endorsement to *Success to Significance*, by Lloyd Reeb (Grand Rapids: Zondervan, 2004), back cover.

9. "Historical Prices S&P 500 ^GSPC," Yahoo! Finance, accessed December 19, 2012, http://finance.yahoo.com/q/hp?s=%5EGSPC&a=11&b=31&c=2007&d=02&e=9&f=2009&g=d&z=66&y=264.

10. "Compass-finances God's way™," accessed December 19, 2012, http://www.compass1.org.

11. Howard Dayton, *Your Money Counts* (Carol Stream: Tyndale House Publishers, 1997), 10.

12. Lloyd Reeb, *From Success to Significance* (Grand Rapids: Zondervan, 2004).

13. John R. Muether, "Money and the Bible," *Christianity Today,* April 1, 1987, accessed March 3, 2013, http://www.christianitytoday.com/ch/1987/issue14/1406.html?start=3.

14. Richard Stearns, *Hole in the Gospel* (Nashville: Thomas Nelson, 2009).

15. "Facts on Induced Abortion in the United States," Guttmacher Institute, accessed November 10, 2013, http://www.guttmacher.org/pubs/fb_induced_abortion.html.

16. "US and World Population Clock," United States Census Bureau, accessed November 10, 2013, http://www.census.gov/popclock/.

17. "Facts on Induced Abortion in the United States," Guttmacher Institute.

18. Mark Zhang, "The Silent Scream (1984)," *The Embryo Project Encyclopedia*, accessed November 10, 2013, http://embryo.asu.edu/pages/silent-scream-1984.

19. Robert T. Zintl and Carolyn Lesh, "Abortion: New Heat Over an Old Issue," *Time,* February 4, 1985.

20. Abby Johnson, *Unplanned* (Tyndale House Publishers & Focus on the Family, 2010).

21. "Who We Are," Planned Parenthood Federation of America, accessed November 10, 2013, http://www.plannedparenthood.org/about-us/who-we-are-4648.htm.

22. Ibid.

23. Daniel James Devine, "News from the front: The top 10 pro-life stories of 2012," *World Magazine*, January 26, 2013, 34.

24. "Injustice Today," International Justice Mission, accessed November 10, 2013, http://www.ijm.org/our-work/injustice-today.

25. "Declaration of Independence," National Archives, accessed

November 10, 2013, http://www.archives.gov/exhibits/charters/declaration_transcript.html.

26. "Other Substance Abuse," National Institute on Alcohol Abuse and Alcoholism, accessed November 10, 2013, http://www.niaaa.nih.gov/alcohol-health/special-populations-co-occurring-disorders/other-substance-abuse.

27. "SAMHSA's Latest National Survey on Drug Use & Health," Students Against Destructive Decisions (SADD), accessed November 10, 2013, http://www.oas.samhsa.gov/nsduh-Latest.htm .

28. Blaise Pascal, *Pensees* (London: Penguin Books, 1995), 148.

29. Kate Kelland, "Smoking Deaths Triple Over Decade," *Reuters US Edition*, accessed November 10, 2013, http://www.reuters.com/article/2012/03/21/us-tobacco-global-deaths-idUSBRE82K0C020120321.

30. Norman L. Geisler with Thomas A. Howe, *Gambling a Bad Bet: You Can't Win for Losing in More Ways Than You Can Imagine* (Grand Rapids: Fleming H. Revell, 1990), 73.

31. Andrea Reuter, "Gambling Addiction Facts & Stats," *Livestrong.com*, accessed November 10, 2013, http://www.livestrong.com/article/119442-gambling-addiction-stats/.

32. Ibid.

33. Rex M. Rogers, "Gambling in America," *Christian Research Institute*, accessed November 10, 2013, article ID DE209, http://www.equip.org/articles/gambling-in-america/.

34. Jerry Ropelato, "Internet Pornography Statistics," *Top-Ten-Reviews*, accessed December 18, 2012, http://internet-filter-review.toptenreviews.com/internet-pornography-statistics.html.

35. Dan Miller, "Poll: Porn Revenues Exceed $5 Billion According to Industry Survey," *XBIZ News Report*, July 25, 2012.

36. "The Staggering Stats of Pornography," Church Mag,

accessed November 10, 2013, http://churchm.ag/porn-stats/.

37. Patrick Fagan, Ph.D., "The Effects of Pornography on Individuals, Marriage, Family and Community," *Family Research Council Research Synthesis*, December 2009, 8.

38. Dr. James Dobson, *Life on the Edge* (Dallas: Word Publishing, 1995).

39. Sheelah Kolhatkar, "Cheating, Incorporated," *Bloomberg Businessweek*, February 10, 2011, accessed November 11, 2013, http://www.businessweek.com/magazine/content/11_08/b 4216060281516.htm.

40. "Ashley Madison," Avid Dating Life, Inc., accessed November 8, 2013, http://www.ashleymadison.com/.

41. "Births, Deaths, Marriages, & Divorces," United States Census Bureau, accessed November 11, 2013, http://www.census.gov/compendia/statab/cats/births_deaths_marriages_divorces.html.

42. Glenn Stanton, "Life Challenges: Divorce," *Focus on the Family*, accessed November 11, 2013, http://www.focusonthefamily.com/lifechallenges/relationship_challenges/divorce.aspx.

43   "November 06, 2012 General Election Results," Washington Secretary of State Sam Reed, last modified November 27, 2012, http://vote.wa.gov/results/20121106/Referendum-Measure-No-74-Concerns-marriage-for-same-sex-couples_ByCounty.html.

44. Ricky Gervais, writer and director, *The Invention of Lying* (Hollywood: Warner Brothers Pictures, 2009).

45. Patricia Brown, "A Question for a Restroom That's Neither Men's Room Nor Women's Room," *New York Times,* March 4, 2005.

46. Doug Pollock, *God Space: Where Spiritual Conversations*

Happen Naturally (Loveland: Group Publishing, 2009), 31.

47. "JC Penney Exec Exits After Sales Tumble," *NBC Today Show Video*, 5:32, televised by NBC on June 20, 2012, posted by NBC News & Sports, June 20, 2012, http://www.nbc.com/news-sports/today-show/2012/06/jc-penney-exec-exits-after-sales-tumble/.

48. Abby Ellin, "JC Penney Raises Ire with Another Gay-Friendly Ad," *ABC News*, June 1 2012, accessed November 11, 2013, http://abcnews.go.com/blogs/business/ 2012/06/jc-penney-comes-out-with-another-gay-friendly-ad/.

49. "The Home Depot Shock Factor," American Family Association, last modified September 8, 2010, http://action.afa.net/Detail.aspx?id=2147498157.

50. "Clearing Up Questions in the News Regarding American Family Association," Ministry Watch, October 19, 2013, accessed November 11, 2013, http://ministrywatch.com/articles/afa.aspx.

51. Anthony Agnello, "The World's Biggest Video Game Market," *Digital Trends US*, December 15, 2012, accessed November 11, 2013, http://www.digitaltrends.com/gaming/us-is-the-worlds-biggest-video-game-market-with-165-million-players/.

52. "Link Between Video Games & Violence?" *CNBC Street Signs Video*, 4:30, televised by CNBC Street Signs on December 18 2012, posted by CNBC on December 18, 2012, http://video.cnbc.com/gallery/?video=3000136265.

53. "Call of Duty®: Black Ops II Grosses $1 Billion in 15 Days," Activision Publishing, Inc., accessed June 23, 2013, http://investor.activision.com/releasedetail.cfm?releaseid=725026.

54. Bill Robinson, *Incarnate Leadership* (Grand Rapids: Zondervan, 2009), 60.

55. "The Performance Costs of Social Screening," ARIS Corporation, 2012.

56. "Saints Versus Sinners in the S&P 500: Cumulative Returns of Stocks Passing BRI Screens vs. Those Failing 1/1/2001 – 3/31/2013," BRI Institute, 2013.

57. "Screen It, Clean It," eVALUEator.com Services LLC, accessed November 11, 2013, https://secure.evalueator.com/MarketingHome.aspx.

58. George Schwartz, *Good Returns: Making Money by Morally Responsible Investing* (Chicago: Geodi Publishing, 2010), 5.

59. Benjamin Graham & David Dodd, *Security Analysis: The Classic 1934 Edition* (New York: The McGraw-Hill Companies, 1996), 230-233.

60. Rusty Leonard, From author's recorded phone interview, December 16, 2012.

61. Lodewijk Otto Petram, "The World's First Stock Exchange: How the Amsterdam Market for Dutch East India Company Shares Became a Modern Securities Market, 1602-1700" (PhD diss., University of Amsterdam, 2011).

62. Mary (Naber) King, "Christ's Returns: Building an Investment Plan Beyond Profit," *Christianity Today*, September 3, 2001.

63. Ibid.

64. John Wesley, Sermon 50 "The Use of Money," in *Sermons on Several Occasions* (Grand Rapids: Christian Classics Ethereal Library, 2009), 515.

65. David Kathman, CFA, "Getting Religion With Faith Based Mutual Funds," *Morningstar Fund Spy*, November 5, 2012.

66. Linsday Gellman, "Investing as a Religious Practice: Faith-based mutual funds incorporate ethical values in selecting securities to own," *Wall Street Journal*, November 3, 2013.

67. Noel James Coulson, primary contributor, "Shariah", *Ency-*

clopedia Britannica, accessed November 11, 2013, http://www.britannica.com/EBchecked/topic/538793/Shariah.

68. "Northwestern Mutual Subsidiaries," The Northwestern Mutual Life Insurance Company, accessed November 11, 2013, http://www.northwesternmutual.com/about-northwestern-mutual/our-company/northwestern-mutual-subsidiaries/default.aspx.

69. "Launch of the Russell-Jadwa Shariah Indexes," Russell Investments, accessed November 11, 2013, http://www.russell.com/us/news/press-release.aspx?link=press-releases/2009/ PR20090624_indexes.htm.

70. "Barna Identifies Seven Paradoxes Regarding America's Faith," The Barna Group, Ltd., December 17, 2002.

71. Abraham H. Maslow, *The Psychology of Science* (New York: Harper & Row, 1966), 15.

72. "Professional Designations: QKA-Qualified Kingdom Advisor," Financial Industry Regulatory Authority (FINRA), accessed November 11, 2013, http://www.finra.org/Investors/ToolsCalculators/ProfessionalDesignations/DesignationsListing/DesignationDetails/pc_QKA.

73. "Diversity & Inclusion," Ameriprise Financial, accessed November 11, 2013, http://www.joinameriprise.com/careers/about/working-at-ameriprise/inclusive-environment.asp.

74. Loran Graham, "SRI, faith-based choices let you invest in your values, issues," *Spokesman Review*, April 6, 2010, accessed November 11, 2013, http://www.spokesman.com/stories/2010/apr/06/sri-faith-based-choices-let-you-invest-in-your/.

75. Chris Herlinger, "Leon Sullivan Dies at 78: Baptist minister led U.S. efforts to hold corporations responsible for investing

in South African apartheid," *Christianity Today*, April 1, 2001, accessed November 11, 2013, http://www.ctlibrary.com/ct/2001/aprilweb-only/4-30-44.0.html.

76. Ibid.

77. Thomas Strobhar, "Battling Corporate Giants and Pro-Life Investing: How You Can Make a Difference," Audio CD (Front Royal: Human Life International, 2008). www.hli.org.

78. Frederick E. Allen, Forbes staff and leadership editor, "Howard Schultz to Anti-Gay Marriage Starbucks Shareholder: 'You Can Sell Your Shares'," *Forbes Leadership Blog*, March 22, 2013 (6:22 p.m.), http://www.forbes.com/sites/frederickallen/2013/03/22/howard-schultz-to-anti-gay-marriage-starbucks-shareholder-you-can-sell-your-shares/.

79. Abraham Lincoln, quote from Lincoln's Cooper Institute Address, February 27, 1860, published by National Park Service, accessed November 11, 2013, http://www.nps.gov/pub_aff/lincoln200/lincoln200.pdf.

80. Thomas Strobhar, "Giving Until It Hurts," *Wall Street Journal,* August 1, 2003.

81. Os Guinness, *The Call* (Nashville: Thomas Nelson, 2003), 29.

82. Matt. 25:23.

CONTACT THE AUTHOR

To get the latest *Investing with Integrity* updates and resources, visit:

investingwithintegrity.net

Loran speaks frequently on the topic of Biblically Responsible Investing and aligning investments to biblical values. He can deliver a keynote version of this content, host a church workshop or seminar, or tailor the message for non-profit organizations, depending on your needs. If you are interested in finding out more, please visit his Speaking page at:

investingwithintegrity.net/speaking

You can also connect with Loran here:

Blog: investingwithintegrity.net/blog
Twitter: Loran_Graham
Facebook: facebook.com/investingwithintegrity